S. J. Hill has it exactly right. Until we discover how loved we are by a gracious Father and learn to enjoy Him as much as He enjoys us, our spiritual life will flounder in our misguided attempts to serve Him out of our own need. Only when we enjoy Him can we grow in communion with Him and be transformed by Him. This book will help you on that journey.

—WAYNE JACOBSEN
AUTHOR OF *HE LOVES ME: LEARNING TO LIVE IN THE FATHER'S AFFECTION*

My friend SJ has given us all a great gift. In his book *Enjoying God* he has helped answer one of life's most important questions: "How does God really feel about me?" With touching personal stories and rock-solid theology, SJ leaves no stone unturned as he unveils the true intent of God's heart. The message of the Father's love, especially in SJ's more than capable hands, is a life changer. Get it today!

—CHRIS DUPRÉ
PASTOR, SPEAKER, WORSHIP LEADER, AND AUTHOR OF *THE WILD LOVE OF GOD*

In *Enjoying God* S. J. Hill has given us a wonderful introduction to intimacy with God. If you're looking to be liberated from the plague of duty-bound, treadmill Christianity and want to know the Lord in a deeper way, this book is a great place to start.

—FRANK VIOLA
AUTHOR OF *FROM ETERNITY TO HERE,
JESUS MANIFESTO,* AND *REVISE US AGAIN*
WWW.FRANKVIOLA.ORG

I loved this book. From the introduction there was a spirit of grace, of intimacy with God, that was ever wooing and drawing me closer to the Lord's heart. I felt, in a way, cleansed, not merely from sin but from serving God from duty rather than joy. This book goes beyond informing to liberating.

—Francis Frangipane
Pastor and author

As much as I am committed to the Great Commission, I am more committed to the Great Commandment. I don't really believe you can fulfill the evangelistic mandate without being a great lover. Great lovers make great laborers in God's kingdom. S. J. Hill teaches you how to cultivate that love relationship with Jesus. I highly recommend this book.

—Ché Ahn
Senior pastor, Harvest Rock Church
Pasadena, California

Do you want to enjoy, experience, and express more of God's presence? This book is your gift from God to enable you to discover and develop a whole new dimension of relationship with Jesus. This isn't hype. It's right here in your hands!

—Larry Tomczak
Author and executive director of
International Center for Evangelism,
Church-Planting and Prayer (ICECAP)

enjoying God

experiencing the love of your heavenly Father

S.J. Hill

foreword by Mike Bickle

CHARISMA
HOUSE

Most CHARISMA HOUSE BOOK GROUP products are available at special quantity discounts for bulk purchase for sales promotions, premiums, fund-raising, and educational needs. For details, write Charisma House Book Group, 600 Rinehart Road, Lake Mary, Florida 32746, or telephone (407) 333-0600.

ENJOYING GOD by S. J. Hill
Published by Charisma House
Charisma Media/Charisma House Book Group
600 Rinehart Road
Lake Mary, Florida 32746
www.charismahouse.com

Unless otherwise noted, Scripture quotations are taken from the Holy Bible, New International Version. Copyright © 1973, 1978, 1984, International Bible Society. Used by permission.

Scripture quotations marked AMP are from the Amplified Bible. Old Testament copyright © 1965, 1987 by the Zondervan Corporation. The Amplified New Testament copyright © 1954, 1958, 1987 by the Lockman Foundation. Used by permission.

Scripture quotations marked KJV are from the King James Version of the Bible.

Scripture quotations marked NKJV are from the New King James Version of the Bible. Copyright © 1979, 1980, 1982 by Thomas Nelson, Inc., publishers. Used by permission.

Cover design by Relevant Solutions (www.relevant-solutions .com)
Design Director: Bill Johnson

Visit the author's website at www.sjhillonline.com. He can also be contacted at stephenhill6@gmail.com.

Library of Congress Control Number: 2012904787
International Standard Book Number: 978-1-61638-614-6
E-book ISBN: 978-1-61638-718-1

Portions of this book were previously published by Relevant Media Group, Inc., ISBN 978-0-588419-774-4, copyright © 2004.

20 21 22 23 24 — 6 5 4 3 2
Printed in the United States of America

This book is dedicated to Jonathan and Lance, my two sons whom I love more than they will ever know, and also to their generation. May the love of the Father so capture their hearts that they will passionately love Him and radically serve Him all of their lives. May they experience the power, presence, and glory of God like no other generation!

Contents

FOREWORD

From the beginning of time there's never been a human being on the planet quite like you. God made you with the shade of your skin. The color of your hair. The individual twinkle in your eye. You are special. He has designed you with the characteristics and personality to touch His heart in a way that no other human being has ever been able to do.

It's a simple truth. But if it doesn't dominate your spirit, then most of what you'll do will come out of duty rather than delight. It will become religious rather than relational. It will produce performance rather than pleasure in God's sight.

Think about it. We live in a society that places constant demands upon our time, energy, and resources. It challenges us to climb to the top. To be the best. To accomplish the most. It applauds accomplishment and is pleased by performance. Unfortunately, these mind-sets not only seep into the church, but they also seep into our spiritual lives.

It's no wonder that the idea of enjoying God and being enjoyed by Him seems foreign. That's why this book is so important. It has the ability to revolutionize your relationship with the Father.

S. J. Hill has unique insights into the affections of God's heart as he addresses this topic. He is an excellent Bible teacher and loves this generation with abandonment. This book is a product of his passion for mentoring young people, and you can feel the intensity in its pages.

Enjoying God will remind you that you're loved for who you are instead of what you do. It teaches that you were created for Someone rather than something. It will challenge you to unleash your passions to the divine romancer—God Himself. It will move you out of your comfort zone.

There is very little time in our world for deep questions, experiences, meditation, and simply waiting on the Lord. *Enjoying God* is one of those rare opportunities. If you'll notice, the chapters are broken down into easy reading portions focusing on various topics, issues, and themes. While they're all related to the larger issue of cultivating intimacy with God, they're designed to stand on their own and be digested in bite-sized portions. Take your time. If a particular passage touches your heart, stop and talk to God about it. Be real. Be honest. Ask Him hard questions. Express your desires, frustrations, and longings. He's been waiting.

—MIKE BICKLE

Mike Bickle is the director of the International House of Prayer in Kansas City, Missouri, and the author of several books, including *Passion for Jesus* and *The Pleasures of Loving God*.

INTRODUCTION

What is the meaning of life? It's a question that has been debated by everyone from philosophers and theologians to college students in their dorm rooms. I believe the Westminster Confession contains the best answer to this age-old issue. Contemplating the reason for man's existence, seventeenth-century theologians concluded that "the chief end of man is to glorify God and to enjoy Him forever."

I remember the first time I read this statement. My heart leaped. There was something about the idea of *enjoying* God that intrigued me. It captured my imagination. For weeks I found myself asking the same burning questions—"Is it possible for someone to truly enjoy God?" "Is this what my heart has been longing for all these years?" These questions kept swirling in my mind.

It was during this time that I read a comment that left an indelible mark on my life. The writer suggested that these theologians were not talking about two different things— glorifying God *and* enjoying Him. He felt the best way to capture the real meaning of this statement was to replace the word *and* with *by*. He concluded that "the chief end of man is to glorify God *by* enjoying Him forever."[1]

God wants to capture your heart. The commitment He wants from you is not the kind you can work up through some sort of spiritual pep rally. It's the kind that is born out of intimacy. It stems from a passionate love that causes men and women to forsake everything for the *ultimate* relationship. Anything less just doesn't satisfy.

I invite you to take a journey with me into God's heart. You will never be the same. It's the journey for which we were created—enjoying God!

God is the original initiator of love. Before you
ever began wanting Him,
He was pursuing you.

the drawing of
the human heart

chapter 1

Have you ever been in love? When you look into the
eyes of the one you love, you realize your priorities
have changed. Time, cost, distance, and sacrifice have a way
of paling when you look at your beloved. Love has a way of
taking you further than you want to go, making you offer
more than you would naturally give, and prompting you
to sacrifice the most precious things you have for the sake
of another. It's both powerful and beautiful. And it was
intended to be that way before the beginning of time.

Life with God was meant to be a love affair of the heart.
It was intended to be a passionate, life-giving relationship
that would make the things of this world appear dull in
comparison. Song of Solomon 8:7 tells us, "Many waters
cannot quench love; rivers cannot wash it away."

When Solomon described love as "unquenchable," he
was speaking of his undying love for a Shulamite maiden.
But through the centuries the Holy Spirit has also used
the language of this verse to awaken the hearts of men and
women to the ardent affections God has for them. It's an
invitation to something that He has instilled in the heart
of every human being. Call it what you may—a vacuum,
hole, pocket, or void—but there exists in everyone a place

1

that longs for love and fulfillment. It's a universal experience. And it's placed in each of us by God, for God.

Consider the Garden of Eden. Can you imagine the intoxicating fragrance of God that Adam and Eve experienced as they walked with Him and enjoyed the beauty of a newly made world? Can you sense the invigorating fulfillment and pleasure in God that they experienced before there was sin? Can you picture the love and passion among the three of them? This was what Adam and Eve were created for: perfect relationship with the Father. They not only felt His presence; they walked in His presence. They experienced Him.

God has placed in everyone a deep-seated desire and hunger for divine fulfillment. We haven't always understood what this was, so we have tried to satisfy the inner craving in a thousand different ways. Yet the fact remains that there is only One who can ultimately satisfy the deepest longings of our hearts.

The great philosopher and Christian Blaise Pascal made this observation: "There once was in man a true happiness of which now remain to him only the mark and empty trace, which he in vain tries to fill from all his surroundings, seeking from things absent the help he does not obtain in things present. But these are all inadequate, because the infinite abyss can only be filled by an infinite and immutable object, that is to say only by God Himself."[1]

Eden is behind you. But the unfolding reality of experiencing and walking with God is awaiting you. The deep ache inside your heart for true fulfillment is really a blessing in disguise. It invites you to something greater than you could ever fathom: the lifelong pursuit of knowing and enjoying God.

THE DRAWING OF GOD'S HEART

Not only do we long to experience uninhibited communion with God, but He also desires our fellowship and wants us to embrace the revelation of His love and passion for us.

You may not realize it, but the Father is ravished by you. You make Him smile. You make Him laugh. You make Him leap for joy. You make His heart beat faster. In Zephaniah 3:17 the Bible even says you make Him sing for joy. Whether you understand that or not doesn't stop God from responding to you in that way. He looks at you and grins. He sees your hair, your skin, your smile, and He rejoices.

The blemishes, scars, and extra pounds may weigh on your heart, but they don't weigh on His. God loves your freckles. He loves your funky-shaped toes. He loves you—just as you are. He loves your uniqueness. He loves the smile that only *your* face can radiate. He loves you when you're awake, vibrant, and full of life. And He loves you when you're down, struggling, and lethargic.

He even loves you when you're sleeping. He gets excited when you wake up—even with morning breath and "sleep" tucked in the corners of your eyes. He can't wait to hear your voice. He looks forward to your first thoughts. He loves accompanying you throughout the day. He enjoys being with you at work. He isn't watching the clock or tapping His foot until five o'clock. Just being with you is enough. He loves talking with you, traveling with you, and being tender with you. He loves watching you enjoy His creation. He smiles when you look at the mountains, sea, or sky and think of Him.

The truth is, God really likes you. In fact, He enjoys you. You may not think you measure up to supermodel or Mr.

GQ status, but He does. Thanks to the gracious act of His Son, He sees you perfectly redeemed.

He isn't tolerating you. He isn't putting up with you. He isn't waiting for you to get older or more mature in your Christian walk before He can love or enjoy you. He loves you right where you are. Through the blood of Jesus you're perfectly redeemed. That means that if you're a tennis player, then you've served an ace. If you're a baseball player, you've hit a home run. If you're a golfer, you've shot a hole in one. Do you get the point? This is what He sees. He's not keeping a record of your mistakes or the times you blew it. His blood takes care of those things. All He sees is you—and He enjoys you. Forever you will make Him ecstatic.

THE INITIATOR OF LOVE

God is the original initiator of love. Before you ever began wanting Him, He was pursuing you. Even while you were still just a bundle of joy in your mother's womb, God was shaping and crafting you to be His own. As you popped out into the world—when you could do nothing more than let out a cry—He began pursuing a relationship with you. The concept of God as the seeker of men and women is made clear throughout Scripture.

For example, in Genesis 15:1 God came to a man by the name of Abram and said, "Do not be afraid, Abram. I am your shield, your very great reward." In verse 5 He promised Abram, "Look up at the heavens and count the stars—if indeed you can count them. . . . So shall your offspring be."

The initiator of love was at it again. He was taking the initiative to woo a man, as well as an entire people, to Himself. Notice that it was God who came to Abram. He revealed Himself to Jacob and apprehended Saul. The names of these men were even changed as a result of God's passionate pursuit of them.

If you study the Scriptures in this light, you'll discover He used almost anything—men, women, babes, prophets, even donkeys—to reveal Himself to people. God also seemed to use any place—a mobile tent, an upper room, a well, a pool, a pile of rocks—to manifest His glory. Apparently He has never been reluctant to invade everyday life to make Himself known to man.

Ezekiel 16:1–14 also describes God's passionate pursuit of a people He chose to represent Him in the earth and usher in the coming of His Son. While these verses powerfully portray God's unique love for Israel, the language also vividly illustrates His intimate affections for all those who belong to Him. His individual touch, care, and passion for them are clearly evident. Even though this is a rather long passage, please take the time to absorb its meaning:

> Son of man, confront Jerusalem with her detestable practices and say, "This is what the Sovereign Lord says to Jerusalem: Your ancestry and birth were in the land of the Canaanites; your father was an Amorite and your mother a Hittite. On the day you were born your cord was not cut, nor were you washed with water to make you clean, nor were you rubbed with salt or wrapped in cloths. No one looked on you with pity or had compassion enough to do any of these things for you. Rather, you were thrown out into the open field, for on the day you were born you were despised.
>
> Then I passed by and saw you kicking about in your blood, and as you lay there in your blood I said to you, "Live!" I made you grow like a plant of the field. You grew up and developed and became the

most beautiful of jewels. Your breasts were formed and your hair grew, you who were naked and bare.

Later I passed by, and when I looked at you and saw that you were old enough for love, I spread the corner of my garment over you and covered your nakedness. I gave you my solemn oath and entered into a covenant with you, declares the Sovereign LORD, and you became mine.

I bathed you with water and washed the blood from you and put ointments on you. I clothed you with an embroidered dress and put leather sandals on you. I dressed you in fine linen and covered you with costly garments. I adorned you with jewelry: I put bracelets on your arms and a necklace around your neck, and I put a ring on your nose, earrings on your ears and a beautiful crown on your head. So you were adorned with gold and silver; your clothes were of fine linen and costly fabric and embroidered cloth. Your food was fine flour, honey and olive oil. You became very beautiful and rose to be a queen. And your fame spread among the nations on account of your beauty, because the splendor I had given you made your beauty perfect, declares the Sovereign LORD.

Look at all that God does for those who are His children. Even while they are helpless and weak, He pours countless vials of love over them. As a Father, He loves, nurtures, and protects them.

The Lord even uses romantic language to describe His actions and affections. Both His words and tender embrace have a way of touching the heart like nothing else. As your Bridegroom, He adorns you with choice jewels and clothes you with fine garments. As Jacob bestowed a coat of many colors on his favorite son, God clothes you with His very best and, as His bride, makes you beautiful.

He removes your unbecoming qualities and replaces them with His splendor. Thus you begin to reflect the heart of the One who can't get enough of you. But what's even more amazing is that He does it all for love. He doesn't demand penance or religious duty. He deeply yearns for your affection, and this is why He invites you into an intimate relationship with Him.

THE WATERSPOUT

In Psalm 42:7 we read, "Deep calleth unto deep at the noise of thy waterspouts: all thy waves and thy billows are gone over me" (KJV). While some other translations use the word *waterfall* instead of *waterspout*, I believe *waterspout* draws a more accurate picture. Have you ever seen one? Being raised in the Midwest, I had never seen one until a few years ago. Naively I thought I had a pulse on what the psalmist was saying in this verse. But God surprised me.

A pastor friend called me and invited me down to speak in several churches in Louisiana. While I was there, I discovered that he had planned a special fishing trip for me. One night my wife and I returned from a meeting around midnight, and at 2:30 a.m. my friend woke me up to get ready for our drive to the Gulf of Mexico. We packed the gear and arrived at the shores of the Gulf at about five in the morning. The weather was lousy, and the fishing was worse. I was tired. It was storming. All I wanted to do was climb back into a warm, dry bed. But Father chose to let me experience something that I will never forget as long as I live.

As I looked out over the water, I noticed an enormous funnel cloud moving in our direction. Based on my background, I thought it was a tornado, but my friend corrected me and told me it was a waterspout. As the words left his mouth, my heart leaped. I thought, "This is awesome!" And I watched it in the distance.

In the midst of those stormy, early morning hours, I had an opportunity to actually see what the psalmist was talking about, and I learned a few lessons. Waterspouts are basically tornadoes that usually occur over large bodies of water. They defy gravity. At the ocean's surface winds gain speed—sometimes close to two hundred miles per hour—swirl into a vortex, and then move upward. In the Florida Keys, where waterspouts occur more frequently than anywhere else in the world, the clouds that spawn the spouts are between eighteen thousand and twenty-two thousand feet high.[2]

Look at the words of Psalm 42:7 again: "Deep calleth unto deep at the noise of thy waterspouts: all thy waves and thy billows are gone over me" (KJV). Now picture a hand reaching down twenty-two thousand feet to touch something inside of you. God is continually calling to that deep place within the human heart as He seeks to manifest Himself to those He loves.

There is a place within you—a deep place—that only God can touch. It's in that place that God's echoing invitation emerges and penetrates your spirit. It's the invitation not only to experience Him but also to enjoy Him. This call comes out of an even deeper place, a deeper longing, in the heart of God. As much as you may want Him, He wants you more.

The Pursuer of the Human Heart

Some people define religion as man's search for God. However, the Bible speaks of God's search for man. The mystery of it all is that God pursues man. When Adam and Eve hid from His presence, the Lord called, "Where are you?" (Gen. 3:9).

It's a call that goes out again and again. You've heard it. It's the echo of a still, small voice that is uniquely mysterious. It transcends words yet continually draws the human spirit.

Over the years various books have been written to challenge people to pursue God, and there is certainly an important place in the Christian experience for wanting to encounter Him in deeper ways. But as you look more closely at Scriptures, you'll discover that God is always the first to initiate love. It's your role to respond.

Any passion you have in your heart for Him right now, He put there. It takes God to love God. It takes God to want God. You didn't just wake up one morning thinking that it would be a good day to give your heart to the Lord. The lover of your heart was pursuing you even when you didn't realize it. He was working behind the scenes, proactive in the circumstances of your life, bringing you to a place where through His grace you could experience Him.

This is both a humbling and profound truth. How can someone who is "blind" to the beauty of God have the scales fall from his eyes and his heart awakened to intimacy apart from the Lord touching and drawing him? While some people say they've known God since they were children and have never really walked away from Him, most of us remember when we were lost and *clueless* about His love.

Even those who came to know the Lord at an early age must admit that, at times, their lifestyles weren't what He intended for them. Think about it. If this scenario applies to you, then at those times you weren't responding to Him as you should have been. Yet He came seeking you. He pursued you. He loved you.

If these truths are stirring something within your heart, then you're not alone. Years ago I taught on this concept at a ministry training school. It was my second semester, and most of the students at the institute had never heard me speak. I was asked to teach an elective that the school called "Cultivating Intimacy With God." More than four hundred students, or approximately one-third of the student body, signed up for the class. That clearly wasn't because of me. It was the title of the class that drew them! The heart yearns to have a relationship with the Father—to know Him and to be enjoyed by Him.

The message of the gospel is what sets it apart from other belief systems. It's what makes Christianity different. Religion is man's attempt to attain a place where God will accept him; Christianity is God coming down to man. It is God Himself taking human form and offering His own life so you might be brought to Him.

HELEN, THE FOUGHT-OVER

There once was a beautiful woman named Helen who lived in the ninth century before Christ. She was the wife of the king of Greece. The king was madly in love with her. One evening Paris, the prince of Troy, came under the cover of night and took Helen away. Paris had fallen in love with Helen and had stolen her from the king of Greece. History tells us that this started the Trojan War. The two kingdoms went to war over one woman. According to tradition, because of the king's great love for Helen, he launched over a thousand ships just to get his wife back. Instead of calling her Helen of Troy, we should call her "Helen the Pursued" or "Helen the Fought-Over."[3]

Few of us have ever felt as pursued as Helen, yet each one of us has arrived in the world longing to be special to someone. As little children we longed to find favor with our parents. We have worked hard to win awards, gain accolades, and feel the tender but firm pat on the back for a job well done. But we haven't always walked away with blue ribbons or the kind words we've needed to hear. Moms were busy. Dads worked long hours. Often, as young boys and girls, we grew up wondering if we would ever be noticed. And the cry of our hearts for affirmation remains.

As we enter the Christian life, few people take us aside and talk to us for the sole purpose of learning something about us. How many people have ever sat down with us and just wanted to know who we really are? Not many. As a result, we pursue our identity in superficial things.

Even in our society identity is usually assessed by what we do—housewife, businessperson, Sunday school teacher, student, doctor—rather than who we really are. So we conclude there is nothing in our hearts that is really worth knowing. It's happened to me. And it's happened to you. Because we haven't felt special, we are left with the inner feeling that something is missing, and somehow we are incomplete.

This is in stark contrast to the experience of Helen of Troy, who was not only told of her value and beauty but also witnessed it as two kingdoms went to war over her. There's no doubt that she felt pursued, loved, and special.

I believe that every Christian is a "Helen of Troy" in God's eyes. Through the finished work of the cross, you are beautiful and of great value to Him. He looks at you and sees someone so special that He has to look again and again and again.

The similarities to Helen of Troy extend beyond the wonder of your physical, emotional, and spiritual makeup. Did you know there is a war being fought over you? There are two sides. There are two kingdoms. And they both are fighting for you. This is both a powerful concept and a harsh reality. The lover of your heart is calling you, wooing you, and pursuing you. He is constantly trying to get your attention, your affections, and your heart. But there is also another kingdom fighting for you. It's the kingdom of darkness. Satan and his cohorts are after you as well. They will entice you with compromise, temporary pleasure, and sin. They will woo you with lesser lovers, false fulfillment, and short-term gain.

Finding the Deepest Pleasures in Him

While the longing for fulfillment and pleasure is a universal human experience designed by God, we should never try to satisfy this longing with anything less than what will provide us with the deepest satisfaction.

Julian of Norwich once prayed, "God, of your goodness give me yourself, for you are enough for me.... If I ask for anything which is less, always I am in want; but only in you do I have everything."[4]

C. S. Lewis, one of the most popular writers of the twentieth century, once said that if you find yourself with a desire that no experience in this world can satisfy, then the most probable explanation is that you were made for another world. Can I tell you something? You were. You were made for another world, another reality. Your greatest happiness, fulfillment, and pleasure will only be found in the heart of God!

We read in Proverbs 20:27 that "the spirit of man is the candle of the Lord" (kjv). A candle is only beeswax until it is lit. It can be highly processed beeswax, but it's beeswax nonetheless. The human spirit, with all its yearnings, remains unfulfilled until it's lit by the divine flame.

Spiritual Boredom

Why does entertainment fascinate the human spirit? Why do certain movies capture our imaginations? It's because there is something in our human fabric that longs to be transported beyond our mundane living. Hollywood tries to grab our dreams and passions through films—drama, adventure, romance—and does a fairly good job. But these are just counterfeits of the real drama, adventure, and romance that are a part of God's design.

One of the biggest problems the church faces right now is spiritual boredom. Why? Because believers were never made for a program, an institution, or a weekly pew-warming ceremony. Christians were never made to be satisfied by a three-point outline that contains just enough advice to get over the "hump" of the week. The human heart was made for passion. It was created for relationship. It was designed to experience the adventure of living life with God.

I believe there is an insatiable desire for adventure in most men. Some women have it too. This desire was placed there by God and was designed to be fulfilled by Him. But instead of letting Him fulfill their deepest desires, many believers try to bury them and just survive. They settle for a lifestyle that falls far short of *Raiders of the Lost Ark*. Their lifestyle often involves a cubicle, a nine-to-five job, and a commute back and forth to work.

Left unsatisfied, the hunger for adventure manifests itself in different forms. Men become sports enthusiasts in their quest for adventure. They track the statistics of major league baseball players, follow the March Madness of college basketball, and with pride wear jerseys bearing the numbers of celebrity athletes. Some become biking enthusiasts or acquire all the latest camping gear for a weekend getaway in the mountains. In essence, they live out their craving for adventure in their off time or through the lives of others. That's one reason stadiums are packed, Monday Night

Football has such a huge following, and the Super Bowl is, well, the Super Bowl.

Just as men were made for adventure, women were made for romance. They long for deep, intimate, heart-dancing relationships. Thus, women read romantic novels, watch romantic movies, and wait for their knight in shining armor to appear. Whether watching a "chick flick" or reading a best-selling novel about the undying love between hero and heroine, most women have a soft spot for story and intrigue. They long for true love and passionate expression. Something deep within women's hearts craves romance.

Some men enjoy romance, and some women seek adventure—so the lines are not hard and fast—but the general stereotypes reverberate loudly. Whether you long for romance or adventure or both, God created those desires. They were instilled within you from the time you were born. The secret is to unleash them in your relationship with the Father. Whether it's a desire for challenging experiences or intimacy—whatever that Spirit-driven desire is—it's meant to be awakened and answered in your experiences with Him.

The Creator of the universe—the One who created things that man has yet to discover—never wanted you to live a life of perpetual boredom. Religion is boring. Living with a holy, "wild" God is exciting. And He does things you don't expect Him to do. Knights in shining armor don't exist, but God does. And He provides you with enough awesome promises, hope, and strength to endure anything and take you anywhere.

God's Invasion

If I were God, I would have *staged* a major light show to usher my Son to Planet Earth. It would have been complete with a booming voice and sound effects—a show that only

God could pull off. And yet He chose to show up as an innocent, defenseless baby!

God is often unpredictable. He loves to invade everyday life. He's passionate and jealous for you and your time. Sometimes He comes to you when you least expect it. He doesn't reveal Himself because you do things the right way or you're a super-saint. He manifests Himself to you even when you're aware of your own shortcomings and feel as if you don't deserve His favor. He does this to remind you that His love and desire for you aren't based on what you do for Him but on who He is. He's deeply moved by you, even in your immaturity. His unpredictable love is meant to fascinate you and captivate your heart with His passion for you. He's not boring. He's adventuresome. He's romantic.

God is always drawing our hearts toward Him. Maybe this is one reason I think about Him a lot and enjoy meditating on the Scriptures. I often find myself reflecting on various verses while I'm walking around the house or driving down the highway. But at times I've had to be careful that I didn't close my eyes. One day I was on my way to a meeting in Ohio, and I got so caught up thinking about the Lord that I actually forgot what I was doing. The next thing I knew, I heard a siren behind me. My car must have been weaving down the road.

When the policeman asked me where I was going, I said, "I'm a minister, and I'm on my way to a meeting. I apologize, but I was praying and got caught up in God and closed my eyes." He looked at me oddly for a moment and then offered a kind rebuke: "Well, just make sure from now on you pray with your eyes open!"

The policeman then proceeded to let me go. Since that experience I've made greater efforts to keep my eyes open when I'm behind the wheel! But what I've discovered is that

God often chooses to manifest Himself in the strangest places—when you're taking out the trash, changing diapers, driving down the highway, sitting in a class, or even watching a movie.

We serve a holy, "wild" God, and He doesn't ask for our consent to invade our lives. He can barge in at any moment. He can completely surprise us. A few years ago I was getting ready to go to Australia for thirteen weeks of ministry and decided to spend some time with the Lord before my departure. I love to walk and pray outside and had found a secluded lake surrounded by lots of trees.

I spent a few hours praying, contemplating God's heart, and sensing His soft presence. I got in the car and began to drive home. Suddenly I encountered God in such a powerful way that I could hardly drive. I had just spent two and a half hours in the woods; He could have touched me there, but He waited until I was in the car driving home. Why? Who knows?

Some of you may struggle with this concept, but I believe God is constantly looking for ways to invade your life. I mean this in a good sense. God will never allow Himself to be put into a nice, neat little box. He is the Father of surprises. And He's ravished by you!

CLOSING PRAYER

Father, stir such a passion in my heart that words cannot describe the adoration I will have for You. Give me a revelation of just how much You love me. Remind me of the times and ways You have pursued me. Increase my desire for You. Ignite the red-hot fires of Your love and unconditional acceptance in my heart so I will be changed forever. Kiss me with the kisses of Your Word. Soften my heart. Liberate me. Bring me into an unfolding understanding of Your heart and Your passion for me. Father, I want to know who You really are. Reveal Yourself to me. Warm my heart with Your Spirit and make me more like Your Son. In Jesus's name. Amen. ♡

The Lord is purely jealous
for His bride, but He's not
jealous on His behalf. He
wants the best for her.

the divine romance

chapter 2

When you first came to Christ, whatever your experience, there was a reason why you opened your heart to Him. Yes, He was seeking you first, but there was something built into your human fabric that caused you to respond. You were looking for warmth. You were looking for love. You were looking for fulfillment. You were looking for relationship. You were looking for an identity beyond your existence.

You were not looking for a program. You were not looking for an institution. You were not looking for a *somewhere* but for a *Someone*. It's sad that over the years the gospel has rarely been depicted as a divine romance. The church's approach to the gospel has often been to reduce it to nothing more than a formula. Some modern methods of evangelism resemble an IRS 1040 form: it has all the information, but it doesn't take your breath away.

Yet the Bible is an invitation to an incredible sacred romance of the heart with the great romancer, God Himself. Like the king of Greece, He's in hot pursuit of those taken from Him. If you will begin to allow this shift in thinking to permeate your heart and mind, then you will start seeing the Scriptures differently. Verses will leap off the pages and come to life like never before. The message of the gospel will open you to a sacred love affair of the heart that will leave you full of hope and with a promise of deep intimacy.

But like Helen of Troy, we won't return to an eternal love affair with our Bridegroom King without a battle. Many of us have carried baggage into our Christian experience that has never been unpacked. Rejection, insecurity, and fear stand against the divine romance in such stark contrast that it's hard for us to fully grasp the heart of the gospel.

While the divine romancer calls us away to a life of wholeness through experiencing His heart, the pain of the past and the things that we've encountered in life suggest to us that we're on our own. They whisper to us that there really is no divine romance and that God is not the magnificent lover of our hearts. Still the romancer persists and invites us to trust. Unfortunately many of us are so full of fear that it's hard to open our hearts to Him. Cases of betrayal replay in the back chambers of our memories, and our pain causes us to remain somewhat aloof and independent.

We're reluctant to open ourselves fully to God because we don't want to become too vulnerable. Can He really be trusted? Does He really want us to experience a superior pleasure and fulfillment in His presence? Were we truly made to enjoy Him?

As you read these questions, does something in the depths of your spirit cry out, "Yes! Yes! Yes!"? Then it's time to get in touch with your heart. It's time to take a moment to respond.

RELATIONSHIP WITH THE DIVINE ROMANCER

When you're first introduced to the divine love story, you discover that it didn't begin in the Garden of Eden. It began with God in relationship. You see, before man was created, the Father was already in relationship with Someone.

In Proverbs 8:27–29 we read, "I was there when he set the heavens in place, when he marked out the horizon on the face of the deep, when he established the clouds above and fixed securely the fountains of the deep, when he gave the sea its boundary so the waters would not overstep his command, and when he marked out the foundations of the earth."

On the surface these verses appear to be speaking of wisdom, but actually they're speaking of Jesus. Look at verses 30–31: "Then I was the craftsman at his side. I was filled with delight day after day, rejoicing always in his presence, rejoicing in his whole world and delighting in mankind." Who was the craftsman? Jesus.

Before and during Creation, the Father and Son were enjoying a relationship with each other. These verses reveal that there was an indescribable love and affection between the two of them. It's hard to fathom. Simply put, during the work of Creation, the Father was not alone. His Son was with Him. He didn't need Creation in order to have something to love or enjoy.

Instead, these verses bring new meaning to the adage that the best things in life are meant to be shared. Perfect love always seeks expression, and so the Father, being perfect love, wanted to share His heart not only with His Son but also with His unique creature called man. Verse 31 tells us that He was "delighting in mankind."

Jesus further illustrated this for us in His high priestly prayer. In John 17:24 He said, "Father, I want those you have given me to be with me where I am, and to see my glory, the glory you have given me because you loved me before the creation of the world." Christ was asking that the unique relationship He had with the Father be shared with human beings. Does this help you realize just how much God desires to be with you?

In *The Confessions of Augustine* the famous theologian

wrote, "I came to love you late, O Beauty so ancient and so new; I came to love you late.... You called me, you shouted to me, you broke past my deafness. You bathed me in your light, you wrapped me in your splendor, you sent my blindness reeling. You gave out such a delightful fragrance, and I drew it in and came breathing hard after you. I tasted, and it made me hunger and thirst; you touched me, and I burned to know your peace."[1]

Do you feel the vibrancy of the relationship Augustine was describing? It was alive. His heart had been warmed by something living and real. He had experienced the romantic, pursuing side of God.

But the greatest demonstration of God's heart for us can be seen in the crucifixion of Jesus. The Father did more than launch a thousand ships to get you back. He gave His unique Son—the One whom He delighted in—even before time began. He gave His best. God Himself came to earth so you could be reconciled to Him and live with Him forever.

Søren Kierkegaard tells the story of a king who fell in love with a humble maiden. "The king was like no other king," writes Philip Yancey, paraphrasing the tale:

> Every statesman trembled before his power. No one dared breathe a word against him, for he had the strength to crush all opponents. And yet this mighty king was melted by love for a humble maiden.
>
> How could he declare his love for her? In an odd sort of way, his kingliness tied his hands. If he brought her to the palace and crowned her head with jewels and clothed her body in royal robes, she would surely not resist—no one dared resist him. But would she love him?
>
> She would say she loved him, of course, but would she truly? Or would she live with him in fear, nursing

a private grief for the life she had left behind? Would she be happy at his side? How could he know?

If he rode to her forest cottage in his royal carriage, with an armed escort waving bright banners, that too would overwhelm her. He did not want a cringing subject. He wanted a lover, an equal. He wanted her to forget that he was a king and she a humble maiden and to let shared love cross the gulf between them.[2]

Kierkegaard concluded, "It is only in love that the unequal can be made equal."[3]

In analyzing this story, John Eldredge writes, "The king clothes himself as a beggar and renounces his throne in order to win her hand. The Incarnation, the life, and death of Jesus, answers once and for all the question, 'What is God's heart toward me?'"[4]

THE BRIDAL PERSPECTIVE IN SCRIPTURE

The divine romance is woven like a thread through the Scriptures. The wedding theme, whether it's between God and Israel or Jesus and the church, echoes throughout the Bible.

For example, in Isaiah 54:5, the Bridegroom God said to Israel His wife, "For your Maker is your husband—the LORD Almighty is his name—the Holy One of Israel is your Redeemer; he is called the God of all the earth."

Again, in Hosea 2:16, God said to Israel, "'In that day,' declares the LORD, 'you will call me "my husband"; you will no longer call me "my master."'" In verses 19–20 He goes on to say, "I will betroth you to me forever; I will betroth you in righteousness and justice, in love and compassion. I will betroth you in faithfulness, and you will acknowledge the LORD."

John the Baptist, the forerunner of Jesus, actually referred to the bridal paradigm of the kingdom of God when announcing the Messiah's arrival. John 3:29–30 says, "The bride belongs to the bridegroom. The friend who attends the bridegroom waits and listens for him, and is full of joy when he hears the bridegroom's voice. That joy is mine, and it is now complete. He must become greater; I must become less."

John the Baptist was the first to recognize Christ on earth as the Bridegroom. He was the first to speak of himself and his personal ministry in this perspective. But he certainly was not the last.

Even Jesus referred to the bridal perspective of the kingdom of God. Prior to the Crucifixion, one of the last parables Jesus taught His disciples was of a wedding banquet given by a father in honor of his son. (See Matthew 22:1–14.)

Paul spoke of Jesus as the Bridegroom of the church in 2 Corinthians 11:2. He said, "I am jealous for you with a godly jealousy. I promised you to one husband, to Christ, so that I might present you as a pure virgin to him."

As a friend of the Bridegroom, Paul viewed his ministry as betrothing the unsaved through conversion to the Bridegroom Jesus and presenting them to Him as a pure bride.

It's also interesting to note that in Revelation 19:6–8 the apostle John heard "what sounded like a great multitude, like the roar of rushing waters and like loud peals of thunder, shouting 'Hallelujah! For our Lord God Almighty reigns. Let us rejoice and be glad and give him glory! For the wedding of the Lamb has come, and his bride has made herself ready. Fine linen, bright and clean, was given her to wear.'"

In this passage John described a time when the bridal paradigm of the kingdom of God would reach its climax with the celebration of the King's wedding.

In his book *The Pleasur...*
writes:

> God's mercy to the w...
> prepared bride. She wil...
> be empowered by holy ...
> God. From her sense ...
> view everything diffe...
> make up the bride of ...
> pleasure in God.... Th...
> different world, a peop... ... ...
> romance.[5]

But to fully appreciate the bridal paradigm of the kingdom, we also need to look at the Book of Ephesians, in which Paul addresses the godly relationships that husbands and wives can experience in Christ: "Wives, submit to your own husbands, as to the Lord. For the husband is head of the wife, as also Christ is head of the church; and He is the Savior of the body. Therefore, just as the church is subject to Christ, so let the wives be to their own husbands in everything. Husbands, love your wives, just as Christ also loved the church and gave Himself for her, that He might sanctify and cleanse her with the washing of water by the word, that He might present her to Himself a glorious church, not having spot or wrinkle or any such thing, but that she should be holy and without blemish. So husbands ought to love their own wives as their own bodies; he who loves his wife loves himself. For no one ever hated his own flesh, but nourishes and cherishes it, just as the Lord does the church" (Eph. 5:22–29, NKJV).

The deeper meaning of Paul's words is somewhat hidden from us until we hear him say, "'For this reason a man shall leave his father and mother and be joined to his wife, and

me one flesh.' This is a great mystery, but I
ng Christ and the church" (vv. 31–32, NKJV).
ooking for a relationship with His people that
he perfect marriage. He wants lovers who will
t to Him from their hearts. He desires a people who
e driven by love rather than by outward form or ritual. He
longs for a lovesick bride. He is looking for those who will
keep themselves unstained by the world and will save themselves for Him.

My wife and I have been married for more than forty years, and during that period of time I have learned a thing or two about a lasting relationship. One of the biggest things I've discovered is that when a woman feels secure, loved, accepted, and nurtured, then she has far less of a problem giving herself to her husband. Intimacy comes naturally. But if her husband is a tyrant or a *Hitler at heart*, then she may go through the motions of loving him, but inwardly she will find it difficult to give herself completely to him.

Over the years I've learned that I can bring out the best in my wife by loving and affirming her. Kind words and deeds can actually produce lasting change in a relationship.

This same principle can especially be seen in the Song of Solomon. The bridegroom continually wooed and affirmed his bride, even in her immaturity and weakness. He used such words as "lovely," "my fair one," and "beautiful" to describe her. His words of love and affirmation released her to be the bride of his dreams. Can you imagine how much more colorful, lively, and endearing are the words God uses to describe you?

Through the poetic, romantic language of Scripture, the Bridegroom God is trying to capture our imagination. He wants to convey to each of us that it's safe to fall into His arms, feel secure, and know that He will cherish and nurture us. He will call us out of our immaturity and weakness and correct us with His love. He will remove areas of sin in our lives so we can enjoy Him as the Husband of our hearts and live with Him forever.

THE BRIDAL PARADIGM

You may be struggling to grasp these concepts. You may have grown up with a different understanding of who God is. I fully understand. I grew up in a denomination that bred insecurity and an unhealthy fear of God. The idea of a passionate, loving relationship with God was foreign to me.

As a teenager I attended a summer camp meeting in upstate New York with my father. There was one particular hellfire-and-brimstone evangelist who aggressively preached against television and other "evils." His message fell in line with the views of my denomination, which tended to focus on external issues rather than issues of the heart. I remember groups within our denomination who wouldn't wear wedding bands or any form of jewelry. Women had to wear their hair up in a certain style, and girls couldn't wear slacks, even when they played sports.

As I was listening to the evangelist recounting the "evils" of bowling, I remember the crowd rallying around his every word. What some of us didn't realize was that the camp meeting site was close to an air force base. At the peak of his altar call a bomber came flying over the meeting site seemingly lower than normal and shook the building at its foundations. I remember walking rather quickly to the front of the gathering, dropping to my knees and repenting in fear because I thought the noise I heard was evidence that Jesus was coming back that very moment.

As I look back, it all seems rather silly, but the unhealthy, fearful concept I had of God sent me running to altars more often than not. Today, a healthy concept of God as my Bridegroom sends me running toward a deeper and more intimate relationship with Him. When we understand that God's consuming fire for His bride is a fire of passion and intimacy rather than a destructive inferno, our perspective changes, and our relationship with Him deepens.

Thomas à Kempis experienced this reality when he wrote, "Whoever loves God knows well the sound of his voice. A loud cry in the ears of God is that burning love of the soul which exclaims, 'My God and my love, you are all mine and I am yours.' Deepen your love in me, O Lord. Let your love possess and raise me above myself with a fervor and wonder beyond imagination. Let me sing the song of love. Let my soul spend itself in your praise, rejoicing for love."[6]

Why is it so important for us to understand the bridal imagery of the kingdom of God? Why is it essential that we open our hearts and minds to these captivating concepts? There is nothing more invigorating to the human spirit than the revelation of a Bridegroom God who has intense, pure, passionate desires for us. Something deeply significant takes place in us when in our weakness and immaturity we feel wanted and pursued. Our lives and emotions are radically transformed as we realize that God longs for us and enjoys us.

THE SINGING GOD

God is extravagant in His affections for us! He continually yearns for us. The psalmist David understood this; in Psalm 139:17–18 he says, "How precious to me are your thoughts, O God! How vast is the sum of them! Were I to count them, they would outnumber the grains of sand. When I awake, I am still with you."

Can you imagine? God is constantly thinking about you. You are always on His mind. His thoughts toward you outnumber the grains of sand on the seashores of the world.

The Bridegroom God is also extremely passionate. He is constantly serenading His bride. Zephaniah 3:17 says, "The LORD your God is with you, he is mighty to save. He will take great delight in you, he will quiet you with his love, he will rejoice over you with singing."

This verse introduces us to a side of God that few of us ever think about. The divine romancer, the Bridegroom, is also the original soloist. In verses 14 and 15, look at how He draws His wife into greater intimacy. He says, "Sing, O Daughter of Zion; shout aloud, O Israel! Be glad and rejoice with all your heart, O Daughter of Jerusalem! The LORD has taken away your punishment, he has turned back your enemy. The LORD, the King of Israel, is with you; never again will you fear any harm."

God is inviting His bride to sing back to Him. Feel the emotions expressed in these verses. There is a gladness and rejoicing that they share.

Singing can do things for the human spirit that words alone cannot accomplish. There is power in song. Singing enables the heart to express deeply felt emotions that mere speaking cannot convey. God is saying to each of us, "I love you more than you can even comprehend. You are My bride, and I love singing over you."

Have you ever been in a service when spontaneous singing broke out in the congregation? That's a beautiful picture of God singing over His people. It's prophetic in nature. Why? Because the spirit of prophecy is the testimony of Jesus. He's singing through His people to His people. God doesn't just think of you. He sings over you, and He will sing over you throughout all eternity. It will be overwhelming! While there's an intense passion within marriage, it's only a weak reflection of the pure, undiluted passion He will lavishly shower upon you. Can you imagine the song He will sing?

Some of you may be having a hard time wrapping your minds around this concept. You may be going through a season in your Christian experience when it seems as if God is silent. You may sense the sweetness of His presence, but He doesn't appear to be saying much of anything. More often than not we interpret this to mean that He's somehow upset with us. We think it's a sign of disapproval or separation. But I believe there are times when even our Bridegroom God steps back and simply admires us. Overcome with emotions for His bride, He is moved beyond words. This may stretch our imaginations, but this is how deeply He cares for us.

THE SONG OF SONGS

The reality of all of this is further reinforced for us in the Song of Solomon. While the story line of the book is about Solomon and his love for a young maiden, Bible scholars agree it's also a *portrait* of God's love for Israel and Christ's love for the church. King Solomon was a type of Christ. Understanding both the natural and allegorical interpretations of this book is essential. They can give us practical instruction for natural marriage as well as help us gain insights into our spiritual marriage to Christ. Both applications of this book will lead us to a greater appreciation of God's heart.

Many Christians have a different perspective of God than the one described in the Song of Solomon. Some of us view

God as a drill sergeant who is always making demands of us and trying to discipline us by allowing difficult things to happen. Others view God as a demanding judge who is always trying to catch us in some secret sin. He never expresses any passion or emotion until we mess up, and then He gets angry with us. Some of us also feel that God is aloof and emotionally distant.

But all of these perceptions of God are contrary to who He really is. For example, in Song of Solomon 4:9 we can hear the passion of God's heart expressed through the words of King Solomon: "You have ravished my heart, my sister, my spouse; you have ravished my heart with one look of your eyes, with one link of your necklace" (NKJV).

Now the word *ravish* in the eleventh edition of *Merriam-Webster's Collegiate Dictionary* means "to overcome with emotion (as joy or delight)." The second edition defines *ravish* as "causing great delight or ecstasy." The Hebrew definition of the word *ravish* is "to overwhelm with emotions of delight because of one who is unusually beautiful or attractive."

It's hard for us to fathom that God's heart could be filled with such extravagant passion for His people. Yet in Song of Solomon 4:9 He describes His own heart as overcome with emotions of delight for even an immature bride.

In verse 10 of the same chapter God further declares His passion for His bride. "How fair is your love, my sister, my spouse [bride]! How much better than wine is your love" (NKJV). He speaks back to her the very statement she spoke to him earlier in the song (Song of Sol. 1:2). She had told him that his love for her was better than anything the world had to offer and more invigorating than wine. And now her Bridegroom God speaks back to her and in essence says, "Your love is more precious to Me than anything I've ever created. I'd rather have your love than anything in the universe."

Again, in Song of Solomon 6:4–5, God says to His bride, "O my love, you are...beautiful....Turn your eyes away from me, for they have overcome me" (NKJV). We have little or no idea what impact our love and devotion have on God's heart. He is overcome by weak, broken people who simply love Him.

Who or what has the power to conquer our Bridegroom King? No one and nothing. But one thing has captured His heart—the loving gaze of His devoted bride.

Can you sense the beat of His heart? Can you feel the pulse of His holy passion? He longs to be with you forever.

If you are a woman, how would you like to be married to a man who continually told you that you were beautiful? In God's eyes it doesn't matter what anyone else thinks about you. All that matters is what He thinks. He wants to capture your heart and imagination with His love so you'll never be the same again. He wants you to be liberated in your spirit so you'll be able to love Him lavishly.

I know that this divine, poetic language is hard for some of us guys to swallow. It feels threatening as it challenges our macho mind-set. I fully understand. Being the bride of Christ, however, transcends one's sex. Guys can be a part of the bride of Christ just as women can be a part of the sons of God. To be the bride means to hold a special place of privilege close to the heart of God. Many men throughout history have walked in this extraordinary place of intimacy with God.

King David was one such man. He was the ultimate warrior. Yet he would come straight from battle with his hands stained with blood only to find his heart longing to experience the beauty of the Lord. (See Psalm 27:4.)

The apostle John was another man who had special insight into the passion of God's heart. Yet at one time he was known as one of the "sons of thunder"—a man who wanted to call down fire from heaven to consume those who were not receptive to Jesus's message. Obviously John had some rough edges in his personality that needed to be smoothed over, but he later came to be known as a disciple who put his head on Jesus's breast.

Both of these men were in touch with their masculinity. For us to think that embracing the bridal paradigm of the kingdom of God is somehow going to sabotage our masculinity only proves that we really don't understand what true manhood is all about. However, the revelation of God as our Bridegroom King will help us to become whole emotionally, as well as experience the destiny He has for each of us.

THE DIVINE KISS OF GOD

When we look at the Song of Solomon allegorically, we discover that the dominant theme of the book is the revelation of the passionate affections in God's personality. An integral part of this theme is the revelation of the divine kiss of God. The kiss of the Bridegroom became the passion and pursuit of the bride's life, and I pray it becomes the passion of each one of us.

When I talk about the kisses of God's mouth, I'm referring to the words that proceed out of His mouth—the Scriptures themselves. The phrase "kiss of God" is not meant to conjure up pictures of God actually kissing us on the lips. The divine kiss is a metaphor for the deepest affections that God can give to the human spirit. The divine kiss is what tenderizes and empowers our hearts to love God extravagantly.

The longing that each of us has to be wholehearted and passionate for God is satisfied by the impartation of the kiss of God to our hearts. Think about it. Deep in our hearts is a longing to be abandoned to God and to know the joy of lovesickness for Him. We were made for this. But it takes God's power for us to love God. It's exhilarating when God gives us the capacity—the kiss—to love Him back.

When you are excited about something, you want to share it with your friends. If you find a great restaurant or a café featuring an exceptional musician or a store with unique products, what is your first reaction? To hide it? To forget about it? No, you tell your friends. You also invite them to come along and enjoy the place with you.

By its very nature the divine kiss empowers you to share God with others. It enables you to run with God—to be yoked together with Him as a partner in service for the fulfillment of the Great Commission, which comes naturally when you're truly enjoying Him.

God has several ways of communicating His kiss to us. The primary way is through meditating on the Scriptures. Have you ever read the Bible and a certain verse jumps off the page at you? It suddenly becomes alive. You may have read the passage a dozen times before, but this time it's fresh. You see something you never saw before. Or you see something you've seen before, but suddenly it's real. This is one of the ways God kisses your heart. He's speaking directly to you. He's speaking life and hope to you. He may even be correcting you about something, but this too is just another expression of His love.

Another way His kiss can come to us is through sermons, songs, or the testimonies of others. It can come through scenes in movies, passages in books, or interactions in everyday life. When we feel our hearts being moved, we are experiencing the kiss of God.

God can also kiss us through prophetic revelation by the Holy Spirit. The revelation may come to us in the form of a dream or vision. Or it may just come to us as an impression on our hearts. These encounters can have a cleansing effect on our lives as they lovingly expose hidden areas of pain. They can also impart to us a new knowledge and understanding of who God is.

The kiss of God can even be communicated to us through the ministry of other people. We can experience His kiss when others pray for us. During these times it's possible to feel His presence resting upon us. Sometimes people can reveal the kiss of God through acts of kindness. And sometimes you can sense His kiss simply in the context of genuine friendship.

However you sense or experience His kiss, it's real. And God is probably kissing your heart more than you even realize.

UNDERSTANDING AN OLD TESTAMENT GOD

While all of us may want to believe that God has these kinds of extravagant feelings for us, there may be some lingering questions that periodically plague our minds and imaginations. For example, what of the specific instances in the Old Testament when it appears that God unleashed devastation and destruction on His rebellious people? Or what about the prophets who served as God's mouthpiece for pronouncing judgment on the wayward? How do these perplexing issues relate to the bridal theme of Scripture?

While I can't begin to thoroughly address such a complex subject in this section of the book, let me mention several things that may help shed some light on these issues. First of all, God had a very unique relationship with Israel. The Old Testament frequently portrayed Him as a husband who continually attempted to woo His adulterous wife back to Himself. God was not only disturbed about her spiritual condition, but He was also in pain over her unfaithfulness.

Second, if you look at prophetic ministry in the Old Testament with the idea of God as the pursuer of His people, then you'll discover that one of the primary motivations for His releasing of prophetic ministry was to call His wayward people to come back to Him.

Romans 2:4 tells us that God's kindness leads to repentance. This is vividly illustrated for us in the life of King David. In 1 Samuel 13:14 David is described as a man after God's own heart. This, of course, was the same man who, as king of Israel, committed adultery with Bathsheba. Sin so blinded David that he went for a period of time without genuinely repenting of his deeds. What made matters worse was the fact that David had Bathsheba's husband, Uriah, killed in battle. But God, in an act of compassion, sent the prophet Nathan to talk to David about his sin. Nathan's words may have seemed harsh, but they were actually a revelation of God's love.

Think about it. If God had allowed David to stay in his sinful condition, who knows what might have happened to him? God stopped David in his tracks, and the scales fell off his spiritual eyes. God granted David repentance, and he was restored.

Third, the judgments depicted in the Scriptures must be seen as God temporarily withdrawing Himself and suspending His mercy. In other words, He *judges* men's sins by reluctantly letting them have what they want (Rom. 1:18–28). While the Lord is the sovereign ruler of the universe, He has to honor the way He has designed things in the created order by permitting human beings the right to choose what they desire, even though He knows there will be calamitous consequences for the wrong decisions they make. Still it *angers* Him that sin and Satan are able to wreak havoc on individuals, as well as on the world. Because He is so intricately involved in human affairs, He even takes responsibility for what He must allow. Although it appears that He is the *source* of violence, He merely allows violent beings to do what they choose. But God's ultimate purpose in suspending His mercy is to bring redemption to those who cry out to Him in their anguish and suffering.

A Jealous Romancer

Why is purity so important to God? One of the primary reasons is expressed in Exodus 34:14: "Do not worship any other god, for the LORD, whose name is Jealous, is a jealous God."

In the Bible the name of a person was a declaration of his or her character. It's interesting that God would name Himself "Jealous." There is something within the nature of God that burns for the love and affection of His people. He is a consuming fire of passion who doesn't want anything destructive coming between Him and His bride. Deuteronomy 4:24 confirms this truth when it says, "For the LORD your God is a consuming fire, a jealous God."

Notice also the following passage from Ezekiel 8:3: "He stretched out what looked like a hand and took me by the hair of my head. The Spirit lifted me up between earth and heaven and in visions of God he took me to Jerusalem, to the entrance to the north gate of the inner court, where the idol that provokes to jealousy stood."

The Israelites had placed an idol at the entrance to the north gate of the temple. They were bowing down and worshiping it. Ezekiel referred to it as the "idol that provokes to jealousy." In the Hebrew language, this phrase literally means "the jealousy that provokes jealousy." This idol aroused such a passionate response from within God's heart that He snatched up Ezekiel by his hair and carried him away to Jerusalem. The Lord seemed to want someone who loved Him and was close to His heart to see firsthand the statue that had aroused Him to jealousy, as well as to feel a measure of the pain He was experiencing as He had to watch what sin was doing to His wife.

It was as if the Lord was saying to Ezekiel, "Look at this pathetic idol that has captured the hearts of My people. They're devoted to it. They're in love with it, not with Me. And they're being seduced and destroyed in the process."

God is extremely emotional. Within the depths of His being He experiences extraordinary passions, including jealousy. If this bothers us, it's only because we don't understand the nature of God's character. At the very core of His personality is an all-consuming fire of love called jealousy. His jealousy is not the by-product of insecurity or mistrust, nor is it destructive. Holy jealousy is an intense passion to protect a love relationship that's priceless and to avenge it when it's fractured. God's holy anger at any threat to this relationship is in direct proportion to the burning fire of His love. This truth helps us understand the declarations of God in the Old Testament that may seem harsh on the surface but are a natural response of His love and concern.

The Lord is purely jealous for His bride, but He's not jealous on His behalf. He wants the best for her. When He sees His bride giving her heart to things that could cause harm, He immediately becomes jealous for her safety.

In his book *The Misunderstood God* Darin Hufford writes, "God is a jealous God, but He is jealous on behalf of you. He is not selfishly jealous as human beings are. His righteous jealousy is actually the opposite of what we understand jealousy to be. Until we understand this principle of God's heart, we will always see Him upside down from what He really is. We have taken the Scriptures that describe Him as a jealous God and have given them a selfish and Satanlike interpretation. It has become so common that we don't even recognize it anymore."[7]

THE CALL TO REPENTANCE

The call to repentance is an invitation for you to experience a greater degree of intimacy with God and to change your way of thinking about His true feelings for you. The heart of repentance isn't about guilt; it's about freedom. Even the conviction of sin is a precious gift from the Father. Do you understand His plan for you? It's one of freedom, redemption, and hope. God doesn't condemn you. He doesn't want you to wallow in your sins. He wants you to yield to the work of conviction in your life and allow the Holy Spirit to bring to the surface anything that has the potential to damage your relationship with Him.

God is after our hearts. It has been the kindness of God that has awakened an element of the church to repentance. It has not been His anger. It has not been His wrath. It has been His kindness.

The cry of Psalm 85:4–7 reveals God's unfolding purpose in calling His people back to Himself: "Restore us again, O God our Savior, and put away your displeasure toward us. Will you be angry with us forever? Will you prolong your anger through all generations? Will you not revive us again, that your people may rejoice in you? Show us your unfailing love, O LORD, and grant us your salvation."

God revives the hearts of His people so they can rejoice in Him. This allows them to experience His love even more and come back to what Christianity is all about—enjoying Him.

During the great Welsh Revival that began in 1904 God's visitation changed the hearts of an entire nation. While the revival was centered in Wales, its impact spanned the globe and provided momentum for the Azusa Street Revival in the United States.

In describing this historic event, Rick Joyner states, "Wave after wave of the Holy Spirit passed over the land. The move so affected the people that they gave up their favorite sport, soccer, without even thinking about it. Working-class men seemed to think and talk only about soccer. Gambling on the games was rampant, and at times it seemed that the whole nation would be in a frenzy over a game. Then the star players were converted and joined the open-air street meetings to testify of the glorious things the Lord had done for them. Soon the players were so captivated with Jesus, they lost interest in the games and the teams disbanded. The stadiums were empty!"[8]

While repentance was a key element of the Welsh revival, the fruit of it was men and women falling in love with Jesus. Individuals were brought to a right relationship with God and to the destiny He had planned for them.

THE ROMANCE OF CHOICE

When God created man, He created him with the freedom of choice. There was a reason why He did this. In order for true love to occur, man had to be free to reject Him.

In his book *Disappointment With God* Philip Yancey writes, "Power can do everything but the most important thing; it cannot control love. . . . In a concentration camp, as so many witnesses have told us, the guards possess nearly unlimited power. By applying force, they can make you renounce your God, curse your family, work without pay, eat human excrement, kill and then bury your closest friend or even your own mother. All this is within their power. Only one thing is not: they cannot force you to love them. . . . The fact that love does not operate according to the rules of power may help explain why God sometimes seems shy to use his power. He created us to love him, but his most impressive displays of miracles—the kind we may secretly long for—do nothing to foster that love."[9]

Yancey goes on to quote Douglas John Hall, who said, "God's problem is not that God *is not able* to do certain things. God's problem is that God loves. Love complicates the life of God as it complicates every life."[10]

Do you realize the "risk" that God took in giving man the gift of free choice? He had given this precious gift to the heavenly host even before He had given it to man. But betrayal invaded the universe when Lucifer wanted center stage. He mounted a rebellion and was cast out of heaven as a result. Yet God chose to become "vulnerable" even after experiencing the rejection and pain of Lucifer's fall. He chose to love again. And He chose to love *you*!

CLOSING PRAYER

Father, I long for and want to experience the depths of Your heart. Spirit of God, do for me what only You can do. Take the scales off of my mind and my eyes. Free my heart to recognize

You as the divine romancer. Help me to recognize Your fingerprints in my life.

I ask that You awaken my heart to get back in touch with my God-placed feelings, passions, and desires for a divine adventure and romance with You. Captivate me, Lord, that I may love You like never before. Take away the fatigue and boredom, and replace it with a holy passion for You. Let me experience the fullness of Your love—which goes beyond height, depth, and length—until I am fully alive in You. In Jesus's name.

The human heart longs to know God and be known by Him.

the wounded heart

chapter 3

Years ago, before leaving on a ministry trip to Australia, I read about a seminary student who was talking to a street-hardened teenager in the city of Melbourne. As the student tried to talk to him about Jesus, the teenager asked pointedly, "What is God like?"

What a loaded question! The seminary student had one chance at sharing the good news with this teenager and felt pressured to come up with just the right response. His mind raced. Reflecting on his recent studies, the young man replied, "He is like a father."

Without hesitation the teenager snapped, "If he's anything like my old man, you can have Him!" Later the student learned from a social worker that the teenager's father had beaten his mother and raped his sister repeatedly. The word *father* had dialed up all kinds of terrible memories, and the door to sharing the gospel had been slammed shut.

This brief interaction vividly illustrates the relationship between the impressions left on us by our earthly fathers and our perceptions of the heavenly Father. Because the teenager had a bad experience with his own father, he was unable to grasp the goodness, kindness, and loving nature of the heavenly Father. Likewise, if you have had a bad experience with your father, then it's not always going to be easy to relate—consciously or subconsciously—to your heavenly Father.

What is God like? How do you perceive Him? How would you answer these questions?

Ideally your experiences with your father should have pointed you to the heart of a greater Father who loves you more than any earthly father ever could. Unfortunately this is not always the case. Maybe you have felt the sting of a clenched fist or recall the haunting, cruel words of a childhood incident. Maybe you still carry the scars from wounds of the past. If so, you are not alone.

Through the years I've had countless people tell me, "I have no problem believing that Jesus loves me, but I can't seem to relate to the heavenly Father." More often than not it's because they were abused when they were growing up or their fathers were never there for them. Many people have grown up without ever hearing their father say "I love you."

If you are one of those individuals, I urge you to take your disappointments, hurts, and wounds to the heavenly Father and allow Him to heal you so you can freely receive His loving embrace.

As you read through the following pages, I encourage you to reflect on your own past. This may not be easy. But sometimes the Holy Spirit has to reveal a wound in your spirit before He can heal it. It may not be pleasant to recall or remember, but it's necessary if the Father is going to heal you as He desires.

The Performance-Oriented Father

Many of us grew up with fathers who were extremely performance oriented. A performance-oriented father is one who expresses his approval only after his child has accomplished something of significance. The pat on the back, the words "well done," or an extra-long embrace are given only after the child has excelled in an area such as education, sports, music, or employment. While our achievements should be recognized and celebrated, they should never be a prerequisite for receiving parental love and affirmation.

Sad to say, this performance-driven mentality can easily spill over into our personal relationship with Christ. Initially, as young Christians, we may sense God's love and experience the simplicity of relationship, but it doesn't take long before we think we're not doing enough. This mind-set ingrained in childhood affects one's adult thought patterns.

Performance-oriented thinking constantly reminds us we can't run hard enough, chase God fast enough, pray enough, or serve enough. This was true of my Christian experience. Although I was raised in a Christian home and attended church regularly, over time I found myself becoming trapped in what I call an "inspiration-condemnation-rededication" cycle.

What complicated the situation was the expectation I placed upon myself. More often than not there was a wide gap between where I thought I should be and where I actually was in my experience.

When I was inspired by a sermon or a radical call to Christian commitment and followed through on it, I felt pretty good about myself. When I was praying and reading my Bible as often as I thought I should, I even believed that God was somewhat pleased with me. But inevitably my level of inspiration and spiritual passion would diminish, and I would immediately be hit with an overwhelming sense of condemnation.

Even when I hadn't done anything wrong, I felt guilty for not doing all the things I believed I should be doing. Satan had a field day with my mind and emotions. I would become spiritually indifferent and fall back into old habits. I ended up despising myself for not being more committed. When I couldn't take any more shame, I would rededicate my life to the Lord, confessing my inconsistency as sin. I would make all kinds of promises to God and resolve to try harder than ever to live for Him.

Yet no matter how hard I tried, I never experienced a lasting peace or intimacy with the Lord. If I read several chapters in the Bible, I felt I should have read more. If I prayed for a certain length of time, it never seemed like enough. The perpetual cycle of "inspiration-condemnation-rededication" was a vicious one.

For many years I thought God accepted me on the basis of what I did for Him. Even though I had been told repeatedly that God loved me, more often than not I felt that He was merely putting up with me. I pictured Him as being continually displeased with me. That's why at times I worked so hard to gain His love and favor. Looking back, I can see how ridiculous it was for me to believe that I could make God accept me and love me more than He already did. When I finally discovered that Christianity was not about routine but relationship, the impact on my life was tremendous. God never wanted my focus to be on performing and producing for Him. He wanted my focus to be on His passion for me and on the beauty of His character. What He was really after was my heart!

Too many Christians measure the success of their spiritual lives by whether they live up to certain rules and expectations. They focus on their performance. They try to live up to the standards others have set for them, but they end up believing they can never do enough. No wonder they feel burned out. When Christians try to live by performance, the outcome is always the same: they discover they can never quite measure up, regardless of how hard they try.

This mind-set affects church life as well. There are committees to serve on, activities to organize, and small groups to join. While there may be nothing wrong with these things, over-involvement in them can easily drive us into overload.

I used to believe that in order to experience success in my Christian life, I had to work harder. But I discovered that the key to spiritual success was not strenuous work but spiritual rest and intimacy with my heavenly Father. True success comes out of an understanding that we are passionately loved by God and are called to be lovers of God.

Now that I have come to recognize the struggles I had in my own life, I can see these same problems in the lives of many other Christians. They feel driven to try to win the Father's love and approval. They fail to realize that He is more committed to them than they will ever be to Him. He's more committed to ensuring that they will live with Him and enjoy Him forever than they could ever imagine.

THE PASSIVE FATHER

In 1996 Christopher Robin Milne died in England. You may recognize the name. His father was the famed children's author A. A. Milne, who named the lead human character in his Winnie the Pooh books after his son.

According to Christopher Robin Milne's obituary, his father spent little time with him. He was too busy making other children laugh and smile through his writing to take time for his son. Christopher died in his seventies, hating his world-renowned father because he failed to live the kind of life he depicted in his books.[1]

Like the younger Milne, some of us grew up with passive fathers. A passive father appears distant and rarely gets involved in the personal affairs of a child's life. He isn't very affectionate and seldom shows his emotions.

We live in a fatherless culture. Approximately twenty-two million children in the United States under the age of twenty-one live with one parent. Eighty-three percent of children who live with one parent live with their mothers. The percentage of children who live with two parents has been declining among all racial and ethnic groups.[2]

Those of us who grew up with fathers who were not actively involved in our lives often have difficulty understanding the Father's love, because we view Him as distant. Our earthly fathers never expressed their love and affection for us or spent quality time with us. They didn't seem to notice our joys, our sorrows, or our achievements. This has led us to believe that our heavenly Father doesn't care about the details of our lives. We then find ourselves running to Him only in an emergency. Our relationship with Him never deepens or becomes intimate, because in the back of our minds we fear that He is not really interested in us.

As a pastor's son I can relate to this somewhat, because my father was so busy with the ministry that we spent very little time together. It wasn't that my father didn't love me; it's just that the ministry took him away from me.

My dad pastored small churches that didn't have big budgets and couldn't hire a large staff. So he pretty much did everything. I can still picture my father down in the basement of our house in Chicago on Saturday nights, running off the bulletin for the next morning's service. On Sundays he preached two messages and taught a Sunday school class. He led the service on Wednesday night and headed up the hospital visitation program.

As a result I grew up with a lot of insecurity and rejection, which led to the rebellion I experienced during my teenage years. This is not an indictment against my father. What else could he do? The ministry demanded it of him. I think this is one of the main reasons pastors' kids sometimes rebel; often the ministry takes fathers away from their children. God never ordained it to be this way. As fathers we need to do what we believe the Lord is calling us to do, but not at the cost of neglecting our families.

The Punitive Father

Some of us also had fathers who were overly strict and stern. They placed demands on us that often broke our spirits. An authoritarian father tends to rule with a mixture of fear and guilt. Instead of offering love and affirmation to his children, he continually points out their faults and mistakes. This type of father believes that if he reminds his children of their faults, they will be motivated to try harder. However, this behavior can eventually lead to emotional and physical abuse.

Years ago I spoke with a man who, as a little boy, was frequently beaten by his father. He told me that his dad would take him down to the basement and "discipline" him by repeatedly hitting him. This man went on to describe how his parents would also go dancing on the weekends, and his father would tie him to the stair rail and leave him there alone for hours until they returned home. Since then his father has become a Christian and they have been reconciled, but some of the emotional scars remained for years. As a result this man had a hard time relating to the love of his heavenly Father.

It's not just fathers who can be abusive. I know a young man who grew up without ever knowing his father; his mother became pregnant out of wedlock and never married. Early in his teenage years his mother told him that she hated him. Even though he later became a Christian, he struggled with rejection and insecurity. His mother continued to be verbally demanding and abusive. He never felt genuinely loved, even by God, until a Christian man came into his life and began loving and "fathering" him in the Lord.

If you grew up with a father or mother who was demanding and abusive, you may have difficulty receiving the love of the heavenly Father; you may tend to think He is always looking for some fault in you. As a result it will be difficult for you to picture Him smiling over you in loving approval.

DOES GOD HAVE A GOOD HEART?

These examples of earthly parents are not meant to be an indictment against our moms and dads. Who knows what kind of parental example they grew up with? The only way these strongholds of rejection and fear can be destroyed in our lives is to come to grips with the inaccurate concepts of God that we still carry in our minds.

The human heart longs to know God and be known by Him. But like a lover who has been wronged, we guard our hearts against future disappointments. We have been betrayed; our church and our family members have disillusioned us. We don't want to go through that with God, so we live guarded Christian lives.

Amid the downward spiral of lukewarm existence there remain haunting questions that echo deep within our minds. Does God really care about me? Can He be trusted? Sadly a lot of Christians mistrust God's heart. They won't admit it, but they continue to follow Him from a distance. It's not because they don't love Him; it's because they are afraid of Him.

These fears can manifest themselves in a number of ways. Maybe it's the fear of not measuring up to God's standard. It may be the fear of not doing enough to please Him. It may even be the fear of abandonment. Certain situations awaken these fears—it's almost like pushing a button—and force them to the surface. The enemy always wants you to live in tormenting fear, but this was never God's design.

Satan goes to great lengths to distort our views of God. When these false concepts take root in our lives, they become strongholds. According to 2 Corinthians 10:4–5, "The weapons we fight with are not the weapons of the world. On the contrary, they have divine power to demolish strongholds. We demolish arguments and every pretension that sets itself up against the knowledge of God, and we take captive every thought to make it obedient to Christ."

What exactly is the apostle Paul referring to when he mentions strongholds? In biblical times a stronghold was generally a fortress with walls designed to provide protection against one's enemies. (See Numbers 13:28; Deuteronomy 1:28.) Other strongholds mentioned in Scripture were nothing more than fortified caves and dens hidden in the mountains. (See Judges 6:2.)

It's not surprising that in addressing the issue of spiritual warfare, Paul used a graphic word like *stronghold*. He used the term to describe any kind of thought pattern that contradicts what God has revealed about Himself in His Word. A stronghold in the mind is any type of thinking that gives Satan a protected place of influence in a person's thought life.

Wrong ideas about God are not automatically flushed from our minds when we are first saved. We must continually reshape our way of thinking through an accurate knowledge of God's heart and character. (See Romans 12:2.) In Colossians 3:10 Paul further instructed us to "put on the new self, which is being renewed in knowledge in the image of its Creator."

Satan's goal is to keep us in the dark about God's true feelings and intentions for us. His battle strategy is to twist our views of God so they end up being inaccurate and flawed. As a result we are held in bondage to habits and addictions rooted in rejection, insecurity, and fear.

Satan attempts to build every stronghold he can in our personalities to keep us from the true knowledge of God. To the degree that he is successful, we will not be healed enough emotionally to embrace the affections of God's heart for us. We will not be able to enjoy an intimate relationship with Him.

If we want our hearts to be captivated by the beauty and splendor of God, we must aggressively attack these demonic strongholds. We must allow the truth of God's Word not only to wash our minds of fleshly, immature ways of thinking but also to tenderize our hearts so we can walk in the freedom of God's love. It's only as we understand how God feels about us that the strongholds of the enemy will be overthrown in our hearts and minds.

First John 4:18 says, "There is no fear in love. But perfect love drives out fear, because fear has to do with punishment." If we are afraid of God, we will live in torment to some degree. However, if we recognize that God's heart is filled with passion for us even in our weakness, we will be catapulted into personal wholeness and spiritual maturity.

When my two sons left home and ventured out on their own, I realized even more how much I loved them. I would think about them all the time. I would call them on the phone just to hear their voices. I would picture in my mind what they looked like. More than once I heard the Lord speak so gently to me, "If you feel this way about your sons, how do you think I feel about you?"

I was often reminded of the words of Jesus in Matthew

7:9–11: "Which of you, if his son asks for bread, will give him a stone? Or if he asks for a fish, will give him a snake? If you, then, though you are evil, know how to give good gifts to your children, how much more will your Father in heaven give good gifts to those who ask him!"

Today, as I was thinking about my sons and reflecting on these experiences, I was so overcome by the love of the Father that I broke down and wept. I realized again that when we, as His children, catch a glimpse of the beauty of His heart, it will ignite such deep passions within us that we will gladly abandon ourselves to Him.

CLOSING PRAYER

Father, I ask that You liberate me from my earthly understanding of You and give me an eternal perspective. Please wash away my misperceptions and misunderstandings, and replace them with a biblical concept of You as Father. Help me to recognize Your love, Your daily involvement, and Your unending kindness and compassion in my life. Awaken my heart to knowing and recognizing You as my Father.

Set me free from the strongholds that have developed in my mind over the years, and give me a fresh revelation of You. Liberate me, Father, in the fullness of Your love. Reveal Yourself to me. I want to know who You really are. I need You. In Jesus's name.

Our identity must be found in God and not in what we do.

the audience of one

chapter 4

A number of years ago I came across the following fable.
It so gripped my heart that I remember it to this day:

In a far and distant land there was a spring of
pure water that had miraculous healing properties.
According to legend, everyone who drank of its waters
was instantly healed of disease. People from around
the countryside and even from distant lands would
travel to drink from the stream. So many people
visited the water source that the townspeople began
establishing businesses to support the multitude of
visitors. Stores sold supplies and wares. Homes were
built. People continued to move into the area. New
sources of commerce emerged, and eventually an
entire city was built.

One day a visitor came to this particular city
looking for the healing stream. Unable to find it or
even a sign pointing to its location, he approached a
resident and asked, "Where is the healing stream I've
heard so much about? How can I find it?" The resident
was somewhat embarrassed. He looked down at the
ground and paused for a moment before responding.

"I don't even know," he replied. "In all of our
activity—our building and moving—we've somehow
lost sight of the healing stream."

This story reflects much of what we see today in the body of Christ. In all of our busyness, activity, and serving, as good as those things may be, many of us have lost sight of our healing stream, Jesus Christ. Instead of continually drinking from His life, we've attempted to quench our spiritual thirst with other things.

Jeremiah 2:13 says, "For My people have committed two evils: They have forsaken Me, the fountain of living waters, and hewn themselves cisterns—broken cisterns that can hold no water" (NKJV).

Religious busyness drives us to develop programs and machinery that propel an institution rather than promote a relationship with the lover of our hearts. It takes away our ability to sit at the feet of Jesus. It opens the door to performance-based faith and undermines what Christ did for us on the cross. It serves as a counterfeit for the authentic life that God has for each of us.

We then begin developing our own substitutes—settling for good rather than God. We begin drinking out of cracked wells and old cisterns until it becomes a way of life. We try to satisfy our hearts with the water of obligation and duty, and yet we remain thirsty for something more.

All too soon we forget the invitation Jesus gave us in John 7:37: "If anyone is thirsty, let him come to me and drink." We assume He no longer calls us through the thirst of our hearts. We lose touch with those deep longings that first beckoned us to come to Christ. Like the Galatian church, whom Paul reprimanded for forgetting why they came to the Lord, we find ourselves seduced into returning to religious externals and to performance as the way of salvation.

Yet something keeps tugging at our hearts, suggesting that there's something missing in all we're doing. The longing makes us uncomfortable because it challenges and threatens the very formula we live by, the programs we support, and the format we try to fit into. We attempt to ignore the feeling altogether by getting more involved in Christian service. We tell ourselves that we're just going through a phase that we'll grow out of eventually.

Others of us try to lose ourselves in our work and the things that define our identity. We end up being tempted to give up on our spiritual hopes and dreams, because our hearts are bound up in the things we have fed them in order to keep them quiet.

Yet the gentle hand of our Father keeps tugging at the strings of our hearts, beckoning us to leave the busyness behind and come away with Him. He gently reminds us that the Christian life is a love affair with Him. It's not about principles and programs or even a code of ethics. It's all about Him!

In John 17:3 we read, "Now this is eternal life: that they may know you, the only true God, and Jesus Christ, whom you have sent." Notice that eternal life is knowing Him, not just serving Him.

Again, in Matthew 22:37–40 Jesus revealed the Father's design for man from the beginning: "'Love the Lord your God with all your heart and with all your soul and with all your mind.' This is the first and greatest commandment. And the second is like it: 'Love your neighbor as yourself.' All the Law and the Prophets hang on these two commandments."

The message of the gospel is meant to free us to love the Father with all our hearts. When we disregard the very core of our faith and try to base our Christian experience exclusively on correct doctrine, duty, and service, our passion becomes crippled and our hearts become divorced from the true meaning of life in God.

When the children of Israel went astray from the Lord

and ended up living in an external, religious world of ritual and performance, God said of them, "These people come near to me with their mouth and honor me with their lips, but their hearts are far from me. Their worship of me is made up only of rules taught by men" (Isa. 29:13).

Listen to the passion of God's heart expressed in Ezekiel 44:15–18: "'But the priests, the Levites, the sons of Zadok, who kept charge of My sanctuary when the children of Israel went astray from Me, they shall come near Me to minister to Me; and they shall stand before Me to offer to Me the fat and the blood,' says the Lord God. 'They shall enter My sanctuary, and they shall come near My table to minister to Me, and they shall keep My charge. And it shall be, whenever they enter the gates of the inner court, that they shall put on linen garments; no wool shall come upon them while they minister within the gates of the inner court or within the house. They shall have linen turbans on their heads and linen trousers on their bodies; they shall not clothe themselves with anything that causes sweat'" (NKJV).

Commenting on this passage in his booklet *Ministering to the House or to God?,* Watchman Nee wrote the following words:

> Work for the Lord undoubtedly has its attractions for the flesh. You may find it very interesting, and you may be thrilled when crowds gather to hear you preach, and when numbers of souls are saved. If you have to stay at home, occupied from morning to night with mundane matters, then you think: How meaningless life is! How grand it would be if I could go out and serve the Lord! If only I were free to go around preaching, or even to talk to people about Him!
>
> But that is not spirituality. Oh, if only we could see that very much work done for God is not really

ministry to Him!...The thing I fear most is that many of you will go out and win sinners to the Lord and build up believers, without ministering to the Lord Himself. Much so-called service for Him is simply following our own natural inclinations. We have such active dispositions that we cannot bear to stay at home, so we run around for our own relief. We may be serving sinners, and we may be serving believers, but we are all the time serving our own flesh.

How hard we often find it to drag ourselves into His presence! We shrink from the solitude, and even when we do detach ourselves physically, our thoughts still keep wandering outside. Many of us can enjoy working among people, but how many of us can draw near to God in the Holy of Holies? Yet it is only as we draw near to Him that we can minister to Him....Unless we really know what it is to draw near to God, we cannot know what it is to serve Him. It is impossible to stand afar off and still minister to Him. We cannot serve Him from a distance.

But such ministry is confined to a certain place, "They shall enter into my sanctuary, and they shall come near to my table, to minister unto me, and they shall keep my charge" (v. 16, KJV). Ministry that is "unto me" is in the inner sanctuary, in the hidden place, not in the outer court exposed to public view. People may think we are doing nothing, but service to God within the Holy Place far transcends service to the people in the outer court.

The same passage tells us how they must be clothed who would minister to the Lord....Those who minister to the Lord may not wear wool. Why not?...No work that produces sweat is acceptable to the Lord. But what does "sweat" signify? We all know that the first occasion when sweat is mentioned was when Adam was driven from the garden of Eden....It is clear that sweat is a condition of the curse. Because the curse rested on the ground it ceased to yield its fruit without man's effort, and such effort produced sweat. When the blessing of God is withheld, fleshly effort becomes necessary, and that causes sweat. All work that produces sweat is positively prohibited to those who minister to the Lord. Yet today what an expenditure of energy there is in work for Him!...Before work for God can be undertaken there is a great deal of rushing to and fro, making numerous contacts, having consultations and discussions, and finally getting the approval of various people before going ahead. As for waiting quietly in the presence of God and seeking His instructions, that is out of the question. Yet in spiritual work the one factor to be taken into account is God. The one Person to make contact with is God.[1]

This principle is reinforced for us even further in Mark 3, where Jesus selected His twelve disciples. In verse 14 Mark wrote, "He appointed twelve—designating them apostles— that they might be with him and that he might send them out to preach."

The sequence of events in this verse is very significant. Jesus appointed the disciples so they could be with Him. Before He sent them out, His primary concern and focus was to nurture them and to develop intimacy with them. They were affirmed in His love, established in a relationship with Him, and then sent out.

Consider the transformation of Saul in his Damascus Road experience. In Acts 9:3–6 the man who had been brutally persecuting the church was confronted with a mysterious light flashing around him, and a voice challenged him, "Saul, Saul, why are you persecuting Me?" (v. 4, NKJV). His response in verse 5, "Who are you, Lord?", is important to note.

While Saul thought he had been defending God, he was confronted with the reality that he really didn't know Him. The Scriptures seem to indicate that shortly after his conversion, he disappeared into Arabia for nearly fourteen years. What was he doing? I believe he was deepening his relationship with God. He spent time with Him so that when he was launched into ministry, he had something to impart to those with whom he came in contact.

In this passage Saul also asked a second question: "Lord, what do You want me to do?" (v. 6, NKJV). Notice the sequence of these two questions. They reflect the priority of God's heart. More often than not, we put the cart before the horse. We reverse the order of these two questions. Having established our identity in the things we do, we find ourselves more concerned about what we can accomplish for the Lord instead of becoming more intimate with Him.

This way of thinking is contrary to the example left for us by the apostles. Addressing the religious leaders of his day, Peter said in Acts 4:9–12, "If we are being called to account today for an act of kindness shown to a cripple and are asked how he was healed, then know this, you and all the people of Israel: It is by the name of Jesus Christ of Nazareth, whom you crucified but whom God raised from the dead, that this man stands before you healed. He is 'the stone you builders rejected, which has become the capstone.' Salvation is found in no one else, for there is no other name under heaven given to men by which we must be saved." Now notice in particular verse 13: "When they saw the courage of Peter and John and realized that they were unschooled, ordinary men, they were astonished and they took note that these men had been with Jesus." The apostles' success in ministry wasn't rooted in education or effort but simply resulted from having been with Jesus. His presence was what made the difference.

SUCCESS IN THE FATHER'S EYES

We have been programmed to believe that a person's success is based on what he does. This view has permeated our culture and even the church. It comes from television, magazines, social position—we are inundated with the message that success is based on performance. One person says, "I'm successful because I'm a medical doctor." Another says, "I'm successful because I'm a lawyer." Another one thinks she's successful because she has invested in the right stocks.

Ministers believe they are successful when their churches or organizations reach a particular size. As Christians we think we're successful when we volunteer a certain amount of our time to the church, donate a particular amount of money to various causes, or have a perfect attendance record at Sunday school.

For some believers success boils down to the number of days they commit to fasting, the number of hours they spend in prayer, or the number of chapters they read in the Bible.

But what is the biblical view of success? As we'll see, it's very different from ours. The stories of success in the Bible aren't four-color glossies of men and women with airbrushed lives. Instead the Scriptures expose the truth, warts and all. They reveal that what makes a man or woman successful is not what they do. In fact, true success is based on the realization that we are loved by God and that we are lovers of God. This is God's definition of success. It reflects God's perspective, not man's.

Psalm 18:35 says, "You give me your shield of victory, and your right hand sustains me; you stoop down to make me great." What makes a person great? The presence of God in that person's life—not his or her accomplishments.

Does something drive you to serve God in order to please Him? If so, you need to realize that you weren't made to find your identity in the things you do. You were made to be in relationship with God. The Father doesn't define your life by what you do. He defines your life by who He created you to be for Himself. He doesn't want your efforts as much as He wants you. He enjoys your worship. He enjoys your dance. He enjoys the times that you think about Him. But most of all He enjoys you.

THE FATHER'S AFFIRMATION OF JESUS

While many of us grew up in performance-oriented homes, the heavenly Father never bases His affirmation of us on what we do for Him. This principle is vividly illustrated for us in the life of Christ. Have you ever noticed how His Father affirmed Him? You may have missed it. It's easy to overlook. It came at the beginning of the Lord's ministry—perhaps much earlier than you'd expect.

Mark 1:9–11 says, "At that time Jesus came from Nazareth in Galilee and was baptized by John in the Jordan. As Jesus was coming up out of the water, he saw heaven being torn open and the Spirit descending on him like a dove. And a voice came from heaven: 'You are my Son, whom I love; with you I am well pleased.'"

Look again at what the Father said to His Son: "You are my Son, whom I love; with you I am well pleased." What incredible words! What a strong affirmation! The Father not only declared publicly that Jesus was His Son but also told Him, in an audible voice, that He loved Him and was pleased with Him.

These were life-impacting words to Jesus. But do you know

what was just as meaningful? *When* the Father spoke them. The Father's affirmation for His Son came at the beginning of Jesus's ministry. He hadn't worked a single miracle, healed any blind eyes, cleansed any lepers, or ruined any funerals. In fact, He hadn't even begun His ministry. Yet the Father was pleased with Him. Why? Because the Father delighted in His Son and Jesus delighted in His Father. They were in relationship.

To fully appreciate what took place, we need to remember that Jesus experienced this as a human being. This powerful affirmation of the Father's love was crucial for Jesus at the beginning of His ministry. This event affected Him significantly.

The Father's love and affirmation were the sources of Jesus's security. He walked the earth with the assurance that He was approved and affirmed in the Father's love. Having the approval of His Father freed Him from having to work for it or for the approval of men. John 6:27 says, "On him God the Father has placed his seal of approval."

The love of the Father also enabled Jesus to love and affirm others. On one occasion Jesus said to His disciples, "You believe at last!...But a time is coming, and has come, when you will be scattered, each to his own home. You will leave me all alone. Yet I am not alone, for my Father is with me. I have told you these things, so that in me you may have peace. In this world you will have trouble. But take heart! I have overcome the world" (John 16:31–33).

I believe the Father's love and approval were pivotal to Jesus's success in life and ministry. They empowered Him in His commitment to His Father. Because of the Father's blessing, Jesus was able to find His identity in their relationship with one another. He didn't need the ministry to experience fulfillment in His life.

THE FATHER'S BLESSING

In their book *The Blessing,* Gary Smalley and John Trent describe different components of the blessing that sons need to receive from their fathers. This book is a valuable one that every father should read.[2]

According to the authors, there are five main parts to the blessing. The first one mentioned is *meaningful touch.* If you will recall, during the baptism of Jesus the Spirit descended upon Him in the form of a dove. This was an expression of meaningful touch. The Holy Spirit brought a powerful touch of the Father's affection to Jesus.

Because of the touch of the Father on His life, Jesus understood the power of touch. This was never more clearly illustrated than in the story of the unnamed leper in Matthew 8:1–4: "When he came down from the mountainside, large crowds followed him. A man with leprosy came and knelt before him and said, 'Lord, if you are willing, you can make me clean.' Jesus reached out his hand and touched the man. 'I am willing,' he said. 'Be clean!' Immediately he was cured of his leprosy. Then Jesus said to him, 'See that you don't tell anyone. But go, show yourself to the priest and offer the gift Moses commanded, as a testimony to them.'"

Notice how Matthew was careful to mention in verse 3 that it was the spoken word of Jesus, not His touch, that healed the man. The leprosy was driven out by a word from Jesus, but the man's loneliness was treated by a touch.

In Scripture the leper represented the ultimate outcast: rejected by those who knew him, avoided by those who didn't, and condemned by society to a future without any hope.

When was the last time the leper had been touched or embraced by another human being? How many years had it been? How many times had he heard the cry "Unclean!" and felt the sting of rejection? Jesus could have simply healed the man with a word.

But He wanted to do more than just heal him. He wanted to affirm him and validate him. Jesus wanted to honor him. Can't we fathers offer the same things to our sons and daughters? The simple act of a gentle touch or a loving embrace can do more to bring wholeness to our children than we can ever imagine. Touch is a powerful means of communication.

The second part of the blessing is an *affirmation or spoken message*. When the Father said, "You are my Son, whom I love" (Mark 1:11), it was an expression of pure acceptance. Those words alone must have melted Jesus's heart. There is power in affirmation. Sadly, most children grow up never experiencing the loving affirmation of their father. For that matter, most family members and friends don't affirm each other the way they should. Many times the people we're the closest to rarely, if ever, hear our love expressed. If we understood the power of affirmation and blessing, we would offer it more frequently. Blessing people has a way of bringing out the best in them.

According to Smalley and Trent, a third aspect of the blessing is *attaching high value* to the one being blessed. When the Father acknowledged Jesus as His Son, His great worth and value were revealed. Likewise fathers need to acknowledge through words and actions the inherent worth of their children.

Fourth, the blessing portrays *a specific future* for the one being blessed. In the Father's blessing of Jesus during His baptism it was clear that Jesus was and always would be His unique Son. The Father powerfully affirmed His future for Him. In the same way a father's blessing will bring encouragement to his child concerning the future God has for him or her.

Finally, the blessing consists of being actively *committed to fulfilling the promise* of the blessing. In the case of Christ we see the Father at work throughout His life, making sure that what had been promised to Him would be fulfilled. Similarly a father who chooses to bless his children must also be committed to doing everything within his power to bring the fullness of the blessing to completion in his children's lives.

These concepts have challenged me as a father. Both of my sons are accomplished musicians who have played with several Christian bands. Some time ago one of my sons told me, "Dad, I'm just not called to the normal Christian music scene. There are a lot of groups out there that relate to young people in the church, but I just don't feel that's what God is calling me to do."

He began talking to me about taking his music to the streets, bars, and clubs. As a minister I know the enormous challenges and temptations he faces by making such a strong stand. But I didn't discourage him, because I believe God has placed this desire in his heart. I know my son's heart. What he was looking for was my affirmation, and I gave it to him.

Many believers try to serve the Lord without having experienced the Father's affirmation and blessing. They know in their minds that God loves them, but that truth hasn't captured their hearts. As a result they are insecure in their relationship with Him.

Maybe you're like that. If so, how do you allow the fullness of the Father's blessing to saturate your heart and mind? By getting to know Him. By understanding His heart and personality. By knowing how He sees you, even in your weakness and immaturity.

Finding Rest

Years ago a student approached me, deeply concerned about her relationship with the Lord. She had made a commitment to get up every morning and begin the day with prayer and Bible reading. These are commendable disciplines. But one morning an emergency arose, and she didn't have time to spend with the Lord. She came to me after class and asked in all innocence, "SJ, do you think God is mad at me because I couldn't spend time with Him this morning?"

This may sound silly to some people, but the possibility was very real to her. I responded tenderly, "It's awesome that you've developed these disciplines, but you need to know how the Father looks at you. You need to know His heart. He's not nervous or anxious about it. He knew this emergency would prevent you from spending the first moments of the day with Him even before you did. He knows you want to spend time with Him, and He loves that. Just continue to enjoy Him and be enjoyed by Him."

Like this young woman, many in the body of Christ believe God's acceptance depends on how faithfully they serve Him. But God's love and acceptance are completely unconditional. You can't do anything to win His approval. He loves you because, in His grace, He has chosen to do so. You are fully accepted by the Father because you are in Christ. Grace can never be repaid. It carries no price tag—not because it's worthless, but because it's priceless.

It's sad that far too many believers still struggle to do all the right things so God will love and accept them. They have grown up believing that a "good" Christian is a person who attends church, reads the Bible, prays, and witnesses to others about Christ. While these things should be an integral part of a believer's experience, they should be the result of intimacy with the Father rather than a means of gaining acceptance.

Disciplining yourself in Christian practices will never produce lasting joy in your life. Too many of you are doing things out of duty rather than delight. You're praying and reading your Bible out of routine rather than relationship. You live with continual guilt, feeling that you aren't doing enough for God. You get up early every morning and try to spend quality time with the Lord, but it's never enough. You memorize portions of Scripture and witness to everything that breathes, but you always come away feeling as if you haven't accomplished enough. You're consumed with what you think you owe God and expend a great deal of energy trying to do more.

No wonder so many of you are exhausted and burned out. Despite all of your efforts to serve God, some of you have even come to the place where you despise the things you're doing. Look at what Jesus had to say about godly service: "Come to me, all you who are weary and burdened, and I will give you rest. Take my yoke upon you and learn from me, for I am gentle and humble in heart, and you will find rest for your souls. For my yoke is easy and my burden is light" (Matt. 11:28–30).

How does your lifestyle compare with the one described in these verses? Jesus actually used the words *rest* and *easy* to describe the Christian life. While He wasn't talking about our circumstances, He was referring to our spiritual perspective. If these words don't describe your lifestyle, then you aren't experiencing the kind of life the Father has for you. If serving God is a chore and is making you miserable, something is wrong!

Martin Luther once said that most Christians have enough religion to feel guilty about their sins but not enough to enjoy life in the Spirit. I know what it's like to try to live the Christian life based on performance, but I also know what it's like to surrender to the love of the Father and allow Him to work the Christian life in me. I've had it both ways. I've walked in both fields. I've been on both sides of the fence.

I've walked in the fields enjoying God, feeling His acceptance, and being motivated to obedience because of His love. I've also strolled through the coarser grasses, feeling a tinge of shame and fear because I never felt I could quite measure up to His standards.

The good news of the gospel is that you can live in the rich land of a vibrant relationship with the Father. The sooner you allow the Spirit of God to give you a clear understanding of His grace, the sooner you can escape the performance trap and experience the Father's affirmation and approval.

Several centuries ago a famous European pianist performed a concert before five thousand people in one of the continent's splendid music halls. He played one of his most popular pieces, and when he had finished, the audience gave him a thunderous standing ovation. Afterward he was asked, "What did it feel like to receive such applause? Was it the greatest experience you ever had?" The pianist replied, "I liked the applause, but it wasn't the most important thing to me. After the audience had sat down, I noticed my teacher of thirty years sitting in the top corner of the balcony. He looked at me and gave me a nod of approval. That one nod from my master brought me more pleasure than the standing ovation of thousands."

The pianist had learned to live before an audience of one. Jesus also lived before an audience of One—His Father.

One nod from His Father was more powerful than all the miracles He had performed. The Father's nod was the only source of approval that Jesus needed.

When we realize that the loving nod of the Father is upon our lives, then we will be free to find our acceptance and identity in Him alone. We too will find ourselves living before an audience of One.

CLOSING PRAYER

Father, I long to know the height and depth of Your love. Reveal Yourself to me in a fresh new way. I ask that You remove the wrong concepts that I have of You as Father and replace them with the reality of Your presence in my life. Free my heart to recognize You as Father.

Wrap Your arms around me until I know nothing but You. I want You to become my everything. I need You. I am tired of performing and responding in fear. I want to know and experience You passionately until You become the One I live and die for. In Jesus's name.

Our success in the Christian life does not primarily consist of what we do for our Father but what He has done for us.

finding our significance

chapter 5

Every one of us came into the world wanting to feel special to someone. This human longing is something we all share. It is an innate desire that we have carried with us from birth. Yet many of us have grown up not knowing what it is to feel valued and treasured by even those closest to us. The dull ache of rejection and loneliness still haunts us as we try to carve out a niche for ourselves in the grand scheme of life.*

Like a cruel taskmaster, the need for significance has driven us to find our worth in our accomplishments or in the approval of others. Some of us have gone to great lengths to try to satisfy this longing. We've become masters at *playing the game* in order to be successful and to win the acceptance of our peers. But, in reality, all we have ended up doing is getting caught on a carousel that never seems to stop.

Several years ago I watched an interview of Hillary Clinton conducted by a news reporter. Mrs. Clinton was being asked about her childhood and some of the factors that had made her a highly motivated individual. She admitted that one of the reasons why she is such a driven

_____

* This chapter is taken from "The Crowning Glory of Our Lives" by S. J. Hill, in *Catching God's Heart*, compiled by Frank DeCenso Jr. (Shippensburg, PA: Destiny Image Publishers, 2010). Used by permission of Destiny Image Publishers, 167 Walnut Bottom Road, Shippensburg, PA 17257, www.destinyimage.com.

person is because of the way she was raised by her father. She reminisced about coming home from school on one occasion, excited to show her dad her report card. When he saw that she had gotten a B in one particular class, instead of praising her and affirming her for her effort, he suggested the school was too easy and wondered, "Why didn't you get an A?"[1] Does Hillary Clinton's experience sound all too familiar?

One of my closest friends is in the American Motorcycle Association Hall of Fame. Steve was inducted into the Hall in 2001. He is the only biker to win the AMA Motocross, the AMA Supercross, and the AMA Superbike nationals. In 1982 he was voted by the American Motorcycle Association as their Professional Athlete of the Year. Steve will always be considered one of the most multitalented riders in the history of motorcycle racing.

Yet Steve struggled for years with a deep-seated insecurity rooted in a nagging sense of insignificance. Looking at his accomplishments in and out of racing, you would have never known it. Steve has also owned a successful real estate investment company and has been involved in a fruitful Christian ministry as well. Still, he never truly felt successful.

Like a lot of us, Steve grew up not experiencing the loving acceptance and affirmation of his earthly father. His dad was *old school*, believing that the best way to motivate his son was by making him think he couldn't do anything good enough. Steve worked hard at motorcycle racing in order to *win* the approval of his father, but he never got it. On the day when Steve was inducted into the Hall of Fame, his dad didn't even tell him he was proud of him.

It wasn't until several years ago that Steve began to understand and experience the wonderful acceptance and affirmation of a greater Father who loved him more than any earthly father ever could. Although the wounds and pain of the past still trouble him at times, Steve is slowly coming to a place of wholeness that he has never known before.

Stories like Steve's are all too common. I hear them everywhere I go. These *father issues* seem to plague the human race. Several years ago I was teaching at a conference near Brisbane, Australia. I was talking about the Father's love and His extravagant affections for us. A couple of days after the conference I was introduced to a very successful businessman who had attended the meetings. He admitted to me that he was having a hard time embracing some of the things I taught because it was difficult for him to believe that God really liked him and enjoyed him for who he was. He proceeded to tell me that he had been raised by a father who, throughout his life, had repeatedly told him he wouldn't amount to anything. As I looked at this man and listened to his story, my heart went out to him. I instinctively knew that he had worked overtime at being successful just to prove his *old man* wrong.

In a perfect world the family unit, and fathers in particular, were to be a reflection of God's unfailing love for His children. But in a world infected by sin, the vicious cycle of rejection has been repeated over and over again. Fathers have passed down to their sons and daughters the pain inflicted on them from early childhood. In turn, the harsh words and callous indifference of dads have ended up crippling children in every generation.

Today, absent fathers (physically and emotionally), abusive fathers, and addicted fathers have created huge problems for societies around the world. For example, in America, 90 percent of all runaway children come from fatherless homes. Sixty-three percent of youth suicides occur as a result of fatherless environments, and 71 percent of all high school dropouts come from fatherless homes.[2] Children reared in fatherless homes are more than twice as likely to become male adolescent delinquents or teen mothers. Furthermore, 83 percent of youth in prison grew up in fatherless homes.[3]

The rampant results of rejection are staggering. The pain of being unwanted and the sense of despair over feeling unloved seem to have a stranglehold on humanity. Loneliness has reached epidemic proportions as man's search for significance continues.

In *The Way to Love* Anthony DeMello wrote:

> Look at your life and see how you have filled its emptiness with people. As a result they have a stranglehold on you. See how they control your behavior by their approval and disapproval. They hold the power to ease your loneliness with their company, to send your spirits soaring with their praise, to bring you down to the depths with their criticism and rejection. Take a look at yourself spending almost every waking moment of your day placating and pleasing people, whether they are living or dead. You live by their norms, conform to their standards, seek their company, desire their love, dread their ridicule, long for their applause, meekly submit to the guilt they lay upon you; you are terrified to go against the fashion in the way you dress or speak or act or even think. And observe how even when you control them you depend on them and are enslaved by them. People have become so much a part of your being that you cannot even imagine living a life that is unaffected or uncontrolled by them.[4]

While the symptoms of rejection may vary in different individuals, the underlying cause is deeply embedded in feelings of insignificance. Teenagers will embrace the latest fashion trends and behavioral patterns of their peers just to feel accepted. Girls will become sexually promiscuous just because they long for the love and affection they didn't receive from their fathers. The desire to feel attractive and special to someone often causes them to confuse sex for love. And young men will strive to become the latest and greatest sports jocks just to win the approval of their fathers and the praise of their peers.

Several years ago a student of mine admitted that it had been hard for him to freely receive the unconditional love of his heavenly Father. What has been the underlying cause? The people who were supposed to love and nurture him as a child ended up hurting him the most. His dad used to tell him that he was stupid, and his school grades took a downward spiral as a result. He so wanted his father's approval that he poured all of his energy into basketball. He became such a good player that he eventually was voted team captain by his peers. Yet his father didn't seem to care and never attended any of his games. Even when he graduated from high school, his dad was conspicuously absent from the ceremony. This young man grew up believing that he really wasn't worth anyone's time and attention, even God's.

As adults we can also find ourselves continually searching for significance in the things we do and in the people we know. It can easily become "second nature" for us to measure our worth by the cars we drive, the degrees on our walls, the homes in which we live, the positions we hold, the relationships we've embraced, the recognition of others, the size of our savings accounts, and our stock portfolios. We can readily deceive ourselves into believing that success of any kind will bring us happiness and fulfillment, but it never does. The emptiness we inevitably experience only reminds us that we can never do enough to really gain the approval of others or to feel good about ourselves.

This emptiness has been a part of the human dilemma ever since man chose to believe Satan's lie. Sin left a gaping hole in the hearts of men and women, and with it came a gnawing sense of loneliness that has tormented the human race from nearly the beginning of time.

It was into this dark abyss of human existence that Jesus would be born. The sting of rejection would play no favorites even when it came to the Son of God. From His birth Jesus was rumored to be an illegitimate child of a delusional teenage girl. The Bible also suggests that there was nothing physically attractive about Him as well (Isa. 53:2). Members of His own family didn't believe in Him until after His resurrection from the dead, and if that wasn't bad enough, He was called a drunkard and a glutton. Religious leaders suspected that He was demonized, and bystanders called Him terrible names. He was also rejected by those He loved, deemed a loser, and crucified as a criminal.

THE FATHER'S LOVING APPROVAL

Yet what enabled Jesus to cope with the emotional trauma that seemed to follow Him like a shadow throughout His life? As we've already seen, He lived out of the *loving approval* of His heavenly Father. As a man living in a world polluted with pain, it was imperative for Jesus to be affirmed by His Father. This is why God, in a booming voice, spoke these powerful words over His Son at His baptism: "You are my Son, whom I love; with you I am well pleased" (Luke 3:22).

In Isaiah 42:1–4 we find a prophetic proclamation concerning Jesus that parallels the powerful affirmation given to Him by His Father: "Here is my servant, whom I uphold, my chosen one in whom I delight. I will put my Spirit on him and he will bring justice to the nations. He will not shout or cry out, or raise his voice in the streets. A bruised reed he will not break, and a smoldering wick he will not snuff out. In faithfulness he will bring forth justice; he will not falter or be discouraged till he establishes justice on earth. In his law the islands will put their hope."

This passage also reinforces the impact the Father's affirmation and approval would have on His Son. According to verse 2, Messiah wouldn't have to "shout or cry out, or raise his voice in the streets" to try to gain men's attention and approval. He wouldn't have to satisfy His own ego through self-promotion because His Father's loving care and affirmation would bring fulfillment to His life and keep Him from needing any false comfort from men.

Isaiah also predicted Messiah wouldn't have to prove His authority through the abuse and control of others. "A bruised reed he will not break, and a smoldering wick he will not snuff out" (v. 3). Because Jesus's security and identity would be established in His Father's love, He wouldn't have to go out of His way to appear powerful by extinguishing the fire that was barely burning in the lives of individuals whom He could just as easily have despised.

It was further promised in verse 3 that "in faithfulness he will bring forth justice." Because Jesus would live out of the Father's approval, He wouldn't have to be subject to religious expediency or build His ministry on political correctness. This is why He would be able to truthfully confront the religious system of His day, as He exposed the hypocrisy and corruption that existed in the hearts of its leaders.

Isaiah also prophesied that Messiah "will not falter or be discouraged till he establishes justice on earth" (v. 4). Discouragement would not be able to overwhelm Him because He would consciously live in His Father's delight.

Because Jesus would be grounded in His Father's affections, His focus would remain steadfast until His ministry was fulfilled.

Yet things would be anything but easy for the promised Messiah. Although He grew up perfectly adjusted emotionally because of the love of His Father, His Sonship would continually be called into question. Even after hearing the powerful affirmation of His Father at His baptism, Jesus found Himself in the desert tempted by Satan. The devil challenged Him to *prove* His Sonship by turning stones into bread, throwing Himself from the pinnacle of the temple to be caught by angels, and embracing the prominence and prestige that would be due Him in accepting the offer of the kingdoms of the world. But Jesus resisted the temptations of success, popularity, and power by living out of His true identity. He didn't have to prove to those around Him that He was worthy of love. In fact, He didn't have to prove anything because He was already the "Beloved of the Father," and that allowed Him to live free from the persuasive ploys of the enemy.

A number of years ago I had the privilege of ministering for two weekends in the New Orleans, Louisiana, area. I had some time off between meetings, and so I retreated to a secluded place that had been provided for me where I could rest and reflect on some things I had been reading. I was specifically drawn to two passages in the Gospel of John. For several days I found myself visiting these verses again and again. It was as if I was on a pilgrimage and the Holy Spirit had prepared a place of solitude for me so He could speak to me about something that would change my life and the way I would approach ministry.

With John as my companion, I set out on the journey and found myself intrigued by two verses he had written in his Gospel—John 13:23 and John 21:20. While they appear to be very similar in nature, together they reiterate a truth that is essential for our emotional and spiritual well-being. In speaking of himself, John wrote, "One of them, the disciple whom Jesus loved, was reclining next to him" (John 13:23). In John 21:20 he further stated that "Peter turned and saw that the disciple whom Jesus loved was following them. (This was the one who had leaned back against Jesus at the supper and had said, 'Lord, who is going to betray you?')" Notice, in both instances John referred to himself as *"the disciple whom Jesus loved."*

John often spoke of having a special, unique relationship with Christ. In fact, on three other occasions he makes reference to being *"the disciple whom Jesus loved"* (John 19:26; 20:2; 21:7). It may appear that John was being a bit egotistical about his close connection with Christ, but in reality that was not the case at all. John wasn't suggesting that he was better than the other disciples. Instead he was speaking out of a personal revelation he had experienced about the all-encompassing, superior love of God. *John understood that he was special to the One who is able to love each of us as if we were His favorite.*

If you could have asked John, "What is your core identity, and from what do you draw your significance?" he would have never replied, "I am an apostle, a minister, a miracle worker." He would have simply said, "I am the one Jesus loves." John understood that he was God's favorite. He knew he was special, not because of his accomplishments in ministry, but because of who loved him. He was the *"beloved of the Father,"* and that became his *true identity* and the crowning glory of his life.

This was the truth the Holy Spirit wanted to instill in my heart and mind during my brief retreat. I was being invited to embrace my core identity as Father's special son, but the concept was somewhat difficult for me to grasp. For years I had struggled with a deep sense of insignificance. I was often lonely growing up and wondered why I had to initiate getting together with the kids in my neighborhood. It was experiences like these that reinforced the rejection I felt and led me to believe that there had to be something wrong with me.

Even after I had been in ministry for some time, I was still haunted by periods of incredible loneliness. I would wonder why I didn't receive more phone calls from the people I had met in my travels whom I had come to love and appreciate. Why was I the one who had to make the calls and pursue the relationships? I also struggled at times with questions about why I wasn't receiving more invitations to travel and minister, and I battled with thoughts that questioned my speaking ability.

There were also occasions when I would watch Christian television and catch myself comparing my ministry to others and wonder why God was seemingly using them more than me. I felt insignificant even to God, and I couldn't understand why He wouldn't give me more opportunities to serve Him. No, it wasn't about having my ego stroked; it was about the rejection I felt and the deep-seated pain I had carried for years.

These were the issues the Holy Spirit was lovingly confronting during my time in Louisiana. I knew He was exposing certain mind-sets and emotional wounds not to shame me but to enable me to live free as His son. He wanted me to know that as much as He loved the things I had done for Him, He delighted in me solely because of who He had made me to be for Himself. My *worth* was not based on my ministry accomplishments but instead on the fact that I was the *"beloved of my Father."*

It was then that I truly understood our success in the Christian life does not primarily consist of what we do for our Father but what He has done for us—the incomprehensible things He has dreamed up and accomplished for us through His Son, Jesus Christ.

Remember, true success in the kingdom of God is not ultimately determined by one's accomplishments; true success is based on the understanding that we are infinitely loved and cherished by God. Jesus came to vividly illustrate the lengths to which the Father would go to restore our worth as His sons and daughters. Our lives are valuable because Christ *stooped* and came down to our level so we could be reconciled to His Father and enjoy Him forever! Our significance will only be found in living and serving out of the reality that we have been called and chosen to be Father's boys and girls.

Years ago I had an experience in Australia that would make this truth become even more real to me. Coping with extreme jetlag from having crossed the dateline and spending countless hours in a plane, my wife and I decided to go to bed early our first night in Brisbane. I was hoping to get some deep sleep, but I tossed and turned all night. As dawn approached, I decided to get out of bed, put on my jogging shoes, and go for a run. I have to be honest—I had ulterior motives for what I was about to do. I had discovered on a previous trip that they make doughnuts in Australia that are worth dying for. In my twisted way of thinking, I concluded that if I "tortured myself" enough and ran a few miles, I could easily justify indulging in some delicious, jelly-filled doughnuts topped with real whipped cream.

So I dragged my tired carcass out the front door and was

immediately enveloped by a beautiful, crisp Australian spring morning. After I had jogged for a few minutes, I decided to stop to catch my breath. As I was standing in the middle of a street in a small subdivision, I had an encounter with the Father's love that will always be etched in my memory. Without sounding "spooky-spiritual," it was as if the Father gently tugged at my heart and spoke these words to me: "Steve, you're My boy!" The moment was both passionate and tender. His words struck such a chord in my heart that I began to sob uncontrollably.

For days after the experience I found myself getting teary-eyed every time I thought about what Father had said to me. I felt like He was reminding me that as much as He loved what I did for Him, it wasn't about that at all. To this day I still believe that this encounter took place before I spoke at my first conference because Father wanted me to know that He simply loved the fact that I was His boy!

In thinking back on my experience, I'm also aware of the fact that this reality may be hard for some of you to embrace. As Christians you have often searched for significance by seeking to serve the Lord in various venues and avenues of ministry. You've believed that God has loved you on the basis of what you have done for Him. But if you would be honest, you have focused so much on your *performance* that you have actually lost much of your *passion* in the process.

Maybe this is also one of the main reasons why approximately 50 percent of the pastors in America drop out of the ministry every year. Instead of living out of the loving acceptance and approval of their heavenly Father, they constantly strive to feel successful by the things they accomplish. Rather than finding their identity as Father's child, they live as orphans, searching for significance in larger buildings, bigger budgets, and growing congregations. Some, out of their own insecurities, even *use* those who work for them merely to fulfill their own destinies. But how many of them end up spiritually and emotionally bankrupt because they become trapped in the destructive web of performance?

Several years ago I was invited to speak at a leaders' retreat in Alabama. I was asked to teach the first session because the man who was in charge of the meetings wanted those who were there to be introduced to the message of *intimacy with God*. As I was speaking on the love of the Father, I noticed that not one of them was taking any notes, and many of them were shuffling their feet and looking down at the ground.

Although I was somewhat surprised by what I was witnessing, it suddenly dawned on me that many of these pastors and leaders were uncomfortable with some of the things I was sharing. For one, I was reminding them that their core identity was not to be found in their ministries but in the fact that they were Father's boys and girls. I also reiterated more than once that God had not called them to be "religious CEOs," but He wanted them to enjoy Him and to serve Him out of an understanding of His enjoyment of them. After the meeting was over, I realized that most of them were simply not used to the intimate language of the message of the Father's love, and they were finding it hard to get in touch with their deepest feelings.

It was interesting to watch the reactions of these same leaders the next morning when the other speaker was introduced. He was a man who had planted several churches, and it was announced that he was going to be teaching on church growth. Almost everyone present was on the edge of their seats as he laid out a seven-point strategy for increasing the size of their churches and ministries. I was a bit shocked by what I was observing as many of them were vigorously taking notes.

At the end of the meeting the guest speaker was surrounded by a number of pastors who wanted to invite him to speak at their churches. This experience only confirmed to me that far too many Christian leaders have been programmed to believe they will only be considered successful when their churches or organizations reach a certain size. As much as I want to see authentic growth with disciples reproduced in our churches, we cannot be driven by the need to define our lives and ministries by our achievements.

Christian leaders must be more than successful fundraisers, administrative geniuses, captivating preachers, or brilliant scholars. True leaders are those who burn with an all-consuming passion for God. To them, power, prestige, and privilege are meaningless compared to knowing and loving Him.

Henri Nouwen once wrote:

> Christian leaders cannot simply be persons who have well-informed opinions about the burning issues of our time. Their leadership must be rooted in the permanent, intimate relationship with the incarnate Word, Jesus, and they need to find there the source for their words, advice, and guidance....when we are securely rooted in personal intimacy with the source of life, it will be possible to remain flexible but relativistic, convinced without being rigid, willing to confront without being offensive, gentle, and forgiving without being soft, and true witnesses without being manipulative.[5]

Somehow, each of us must dare to believe that our Father doesn't desire our service nearly as much as He desires us. He is inviting us to celebrate His passion for us and all that

He has provided through Jesus. He wants us to find our approval through the cross (Eph. 1:6) rather than seeking to win His approval by what we do.

This is primarily what Jesus was referring to when He said, "Unless your righteousness surpasses that of the Pharisees and the teachers of the law, you will certainly not enter the kingdom of heaven" (Matt. 5:20). Initially, when we read such a verse, we automatically assume that Christ is calling us to do more. But just the opposite is true. Having come to fulfill the Law (the Torah), Jesus knew we couldn't measure up to its standards. The Law was given to remind men that they could never do enough to be accepted by God. To have a righteousness that exceeds the righteousness (self-effort) of the scribes and Pharisees means we must always acknowledge our spiritual bankruptcy apart from God's grace (Matt. 5:3), actively resist every temptation to base our relationship with God on personal discipline, and aggressively embrace the righteousness of Christ as a free gift.

Because of the finished work of the cross, you, as a believer, now have the same standing with the Father that Jesus has. No longer do you have to be afraid of not measuring up (Rom. 8:15). The Christian life has never been about that. Christ's sacrifice and commitment to you guarantee that you are perfectly redeemed; therefore, you can lavishly obey and serve Him as a response of love. This is at the heart of what Jesus said in Matthew 5:48: "Therefore you shall be perfect, just as your Father in heaven is perfect" (NKJV). Obedience motivated by a fear of not measuring up or a fear of punishment is not the kind of obedience that pleases the Lord. Jesus deserves so much better and wants our obedience to be based on our affections for Him.

I am reminded of a quote that I saw in a day calendar— it was by Max Lucado taken from his book *Come Thirsty*.

He wrote, "With perfect knowledge of the past and perfect vision of the future, God loves you perfectly in spite of both. Perfect love can handle your fear of judgment."[6]

Several years ago a former student of mine sent me an e-mail describing some of the struggles she had gone through one morning during her quiet time with the Lord. She mentioned feeling like a *worm* because she believed she should be a better Christian after serving Him for a number of years. After having spent considerable time repenting for her lack of commitment and asking the Lord to change her, she sensed Him say to her, "Why do you see our times together as a means to an end? This is the end for Me. Our times together are what I died for."

You are special to God! There has never been or ever will be another person quite like you. You are not an accident. Father uniquely made you for Himself (Ps. 139:13–14), and you bring Him delight in a way no other human being can! His lavish love for you is the crowning glory of your life on the earth!

CLOSING PRAYER

Father, I'm tired of searching for significance and success in the things I do, even in the things I do for You. I don't want to keep chasing pipe dreams only to be sorely disappointed. I want my identity to be rooted in Your loving acceptance of me so I am no longer trying to find my worth in what I accomplish. Release me from the rejection and loneliness that still haunt me. I long to experience Your lavish affections for me. I want to feel valued and treasured by You. Enable me to fully open my heart to You so I can be healed and live free as Your child! In Jesus's name.

It is the awe and fascination of the Father that bring us close to His heart.

the affectionate and
approachable father

chapter 6

In his book *Finding Friendship With God* Floyd McClung
shares a powerful story of the profound effect God's love
can have on the hearts and minds of men and women.
Here's the account of a most unusual adoption:

> During the Korean War, a pastor in a small rural
> village awoke one morning to find that his young
> son, his only child, had been killed. Apparently some
> soldiers had slipped in during the night and randomly
> executed a number of villagers in a brutal act of
> terrorism.
>
> The pastor was beside himself with grief. He had
> looked forward to his son someday following in his
> footsteps and becoming a pastor. Now his friends
> feared for his emotional stability, so severe was the
> grief he experienced over the boy's senseless death. It
> seemed so cruel, so unjust. His son was not in the
> army; he posed no threat to anyone. Why should he
> have been singled out like this?
>
> Finally the Korean pastor decided what he must do
> in return for this act of violence. He announced that
> he would hunt down the men who had killed his son
> and would not give up until he had found them. No
> obstacle would stand in his way, no hardship would

deter him. This grief-stricken father resolved to do whatever it took.

Amazingly, he was able to learn the identities of the two terrorists, slip behind enemy lines, and find out where they lived. Early one morning he stole into their house and confronted them. The pastor told them who he was and that he knew they had murdered his son. "You owe me a debt," he said to them. "I have come to collect it."

The two men were obviously expecting to be killed in retaliation. But the pastor's next words astonished them. "You have taken my son," he said, "and now I want you to become my sons in his place."

The pastor stayed with them for several days, until he was able to persuade them to come with him. In time he adopted them as his legal sons. He loved them and cared for them. They became Christians, went to seminary, and were ordained. Today, those two men are pastors in Korea—all because of a father who was willing to do whatever it took to win them, whose love was utterly unstoppable.[1]

This is not only an amazing story, but it's also a portrait of the Father's heart. It expresses His ultimate intention for you. The Father isn't passive in His thoughts toward you or His dealings with you. He has not only forgiven you of your sins and chosen to love you unconditionally, but He has also adopted you into His family as one of His children.

Romans 8:14–16 says, "For as many as are led by the Spirit of God, these are sons of God. For you did not receive the spirit of bondage again to fear, but you received the Spirit of adoption by whom we cry out, 'Abba, Father.' The Spirit Himself bears witness with our spirit that we are children of God" (NKJV).

Do you grasp the meaning of these verses? God hasn't

just saved you from your sins. He has redeemed you so you can be a part of His family forever. When you gave your heart to Jesus, you received the spirit of adoption so you could cry out with confidence, "Abba! Father!" The word *abba* is equivalent to the word *papa* and carries with it the idea of intimacy, dependency, and vulnerability. The concept of God as *abba* was a revolutionary one at the time Paul wrote this.

Drawing on his experience with Greco-Roman law, Paul used the analogy of adoption to describe the Christian's relationship and position with God. The legal status of a son in early Roman times was not much better than that of a slave. A son was the property of his father. A father was entitled to his son's wages. A father could transfer ownership of his son at will and, under certain circumstances, even have him put to death.

In contrast, the legal status of an adopted son actually put him in a more secure place than that of a son born into the family. He was no longer legally bound to old debts, and if he was a slave, he was set free the moment he was adopted. He had complete access to the father of the family and was guaranteed a position in the family as well.

When we first come to Christ, we are given a new heart with new affections. Also, through the Father's plan of adoption, we are given a new status as His sons and daughters. We are guaranteed all the rights and privileges associated with the Father's family.

Commenting on the experiential nature of Paul's statement in Romans 8:15, Martyn Lloyd-Jones said: "What the Apostle is emphasizing here is that not only must we believe this doctrine, and accept it with our minds, but we must also be conscious of it, and feel it; there must be the Spirit of Adoption in us as a result of this work of the Holy Spirit."

Lloyd-Jones went on to say, "Paul is really telling us that we are to feel—and I am emphasizing feeling—in this sense, what our Lord Himself felt."[2]

In other words, we can experience the same intimacy with the Father that Jesus did. In John 17:26 Jesus reinforced this truth for us when He prayed, "I have made you known to them, and will continue to make you known in order that the love you have for me may be in them and that I myself may be in them." What a prayer! Yet it was more than that. It was a profound expression of adoption, affirmation, and acceptance all rolled into one.

Think about it. You can call God "Abba" just as Jesus did. Like a child, you can crawl up into "Abba's lap" and experience the warmth and security of His loving embrace. You can know the pleasure of His heart as you allow your emotions to be bathed in the revelation of His love for you.

Lloyd-Jones added, "The ultimate object of salvation is not merely to keep us from hell, not merely to deliver us from certain sins; it is so that we may enjoy 'adoption,' and that we may become 'the children of God' and 'joint heirs with Christ.' This is what is offered us in the Gospel of our Lord and Savior Jesus Christ. God forbid that any of us should stop at any point short of it!"[3]

THE AFFECTIONATE FATHER

In 1821 the great American evangelist Charles Finney had an encounter with the Lord that radically changed his life. In recalling the experience, he wrote:

> I returned to the front office, and found the fire that I had made of large wood was nearly burned out. But as I turned and was about to take a seat by the fire, I received a mighty baptism of the Holy Ghost. Without any expectation of it, without ever having

the thought in my mind that there was any such thing for me, without any recollection that I had ever heard anything mentioned by a person in the world, the Holy Ghost descended on me in a manner that seemed to go through me, body and soul. I could feel the impression, like a wave of electricity going through me. Indeed it seemed to come in waves and waves of liquid love; for I could not express it any other way. It seemed like the very breath of God. I can recollect distinctly that it seemed to fan me, like immense wings.[4]

Finney went on to say:

No words could express the wonderful love that was shed abroad in my heart. I wept aloud with joy and love; and I do not know but I should say, I literally bellowed out unutterable gushings of my heart. The waves came over me, and over me, one after the other, until I recollect I cried out, 'I shall die if these waves continue to pass over me.' I said, 'Lord, I cannot bear any more;' yet I had no fear of death.[5]

Look at the language Finney used. He compared the experience of God's passion and presence to "waves of liquid love." It came out of nowhere. God overwhelmed him. The lover of his heart was obviously pursuing him.

D. L. Moody, another well-known evangelist, had a similar experience with God during a trip to New York to seek donations to help victims of the Chicago fire. "My heart was not in the work of begging...I could not appeal. I was crying all the time that God would fill me with His Spirit. Well, one day, in the city of New York—oh, what a day!—I cannot describe it, I seldom refer to it; it is almost too sacred an experience of His love that I had to ask to stay His hand.

I went to preaching again. The sermons were not different; I did not present any new truths; and yet hundreds were converted. I would not now be placed back where I was before that blessed experience if you should give me all the world—it would be as the small dust of the balance."[6]

In these divine encounters both men testified to feeling God's love in an unexpected, impossible-to-contain manner. They were exposed to the intense passion of the Father's affection, and it motivated them to love and serve Him more.

Do you know that God wants to bare His heart to you? He wants to whet your appetite for a deeper relationship with Him. He wants to apprehend your life so you can know above all else that you were created for Him.

THE FATHER'S PASSION

It's both humbling and overwhelming to realize to what lengths God went to capture our hearts. He allowed His only Son to take human form and die a brutal, torture-filled death for us. Why? The sacrifice of His Son would not only bring Him the greatest glory, but it would also demonstrate His awesome passion for us. He wanted us to be reconciled to Him.

Many of us have heard the story of Christ's crucifixion so many times that it now fails to capture our hearts and imaginations. But the final hours of Jesus's life were both repulsive and romantic. Christ wanted His bride so much that He gave up His life for her and then came back to life so He could live with her forever.

In the thought-provoking article "A Physician Testifies About the Crucifixion," C. Truman Davis describes from a medical perspective what Christ suffered. He walks us

through the entire torturous experience of Christ's crucifixion to help us capture the sights and sounds of that horrible event:

> After the arrest in the middle of the night, Jesus was
> brought before the Sanhedrin and Caiaphas, the
> High Priest; it is here that the first physical trauma
> was inflicted. A soldier struck Jesus across the face for
> remaining silent when questioned by Caiaphas. The
> palace guards then blindfolded Him and mockingly
> taunted Him to identify them as they each passed by,
> spat on Him, and struck Him in the face.
>
> In the early morning, Jesus, battered and bruised,
> dehydrated, and exhausted from a sleepless night,
> is taken across Jerusalem to the Praetorium of the
> Fortress Antonia, the seat of government of the
> Procurator of Judea, Pontius Pilate....
>
> Preparations for the scourging are carried out. The
> prisoner is stripped of His clothing and His hands tied
> to a post above His head.... The Roman legionnaire
> steps forward with the *flagrum* (or *flaggellum*) in his
> hand. This is a short whip consisting of several heavy,
> leather thongs with two small balls of lead attached
> near the ends of each. The heavy whip is brought down
> with full force again and again across Jesus' shoulders,
> back, and legs. At first the heavy thongs cut through
> the skin only. Then, as the blows continue, they cut
> deeper into the subcutaneous tissues, producing first
> an oozing blood from the capillaries and veins of
> the skin, and finally spurting arterial bleeding from
> vessels in the underlying muscles.
>
> The small balls of lead first produce large, deep
> bruises which are broken open by subsequent blows.
> Finally the skin of the back is hanging in long ribbons
> and the entire area is an unrecognizable mass of
> torn, bleeding tissue. When it is determined by the

centurion in charge that the prisoner is near death, the beating is finally stopped.

The half-fainting Jesus is then untied and allowed to slump to the stone pavement, wet with His own blood. The Roman soldiers see a great joke in this provincial Jew claiming to be a king. They throw a robe across His shoulders and place a stick in His hand for a scepter. They still need a crown to make their travesty complete. A small bundle of flexible branches covered with long thorns (commonly used for firewood) are plaited into a shape of a crown, and this is pressed into His scalp. Again there is copious bleeding (the scalp being one of the most vascular areas of the body).

After mocking Him and striking Him across the face, the soldiers take the stick from His hand and strike Him across the head, driving the thorns deeper into His scalp. Finally, they tire of their sadistic sport and the robe is torn from His back. This had already become adherent to the clots of blood and serum in the wounds, and its removal causes excruciating pain, just as in the careless removal of a surgical bandage, and almost as though He were again being whipped— and the wounds once more begin to bleed.[7]

It's upon His mutilated back that Jesus now carries the heavy wooden beam that will become a part of His cross. The weight of it—just over a hundred pounds—is too much for Him, and He falls. He tries to get up, but His muscles have been pushed beyond their limits. Simon of Cyrene, a North African, is chosen to carry the crossbeam. Jesus follows, still bleeding and in shock. When the trek to Golgotha is finally completed, Jesus is again stripped, except for a loincloth. He is thrown back on the wood of the cross, and a large iron nail is driven into both His wrists and the arches of His feet. Jesus is now suspended between heaven and earth. Davis continues:

> The victim is now crucified. As He slowly sags down with more weight on the nails in the wrists, excruciating pain shoots along the fingers and up the arms to explode in the brain—the nails in the wrists are putting pressure on the median nerves. As He pushes Himself upward to avoid this stretching torment, He places His full weight on the nail through His feet. Again there is the searing agony of the nail tearing through the nerves between the metatarsal bones of the feet.
>
> At this point, as the arms fatigue, great waves of cramps sweep over the muscles, knotting them in deep, relentless, throbbing pain....
>
> Hours of limitless pain, cycles of twisting, joint-rending cramps, intermittent partial asphyxiation, searing pain as tissue is torn from His lacerated back as He moves up and down against the rough timber. Then another agony begins...a terrible crushing pain deep in the chest as the pericardium slowly fills with serum and begins to compress the heart....
>
> It is now almost over. The loss of tissue fluids has reached a critical level; the compressed heart is struggling to pump heavy, thick, sluggish blood into the tissues; the tortured lungs are making a frantic effort to gasp in small gulps of air. The markedly dehydrated tissues send their flood of stimuli to the brain....
>
> With one last surge of strength, He once again presses His torn feet against the nail, straightens His legs, takes a deeper breath, and utters His seventh and last cry, "Father! Into Thy hands I commit My spirit."...
>
> Thus we have had our glimpse—including the

medical evidence—of that epitome of evil which man
has exhibited toward Man and toward God. It has
been a terrible sight, amd more than enough to leave
us despondent and depressed. How grateful we can be
that we have the great sequel in the infinite mercy of
God toward man.[8]

Think of it! While Jesus was suffering all of this, you were
on His mind. He did this as an act of love. Certainly it was
an act of sacrifice, but it was also an act of supreme passion.
What greater act of love could there be than to lay down
one's life? First John 3:16 says, "This is how we know what
love is: Jesus Christ laid down his life for us." And John
15:13 says, "Greater love has no one than this, that he lay
down his life for his friends."

In many ways the Crucifixion is the climax of the divine
romance. Once you embrace the revelation of the finished
work of the cross, you'll never be the same. It will truly melt
your heart.

EMBRACING THE FATHER'S LOVE

At times Jesus used extreme illustrations to enforce the
truth that was burning in His heart. Other than the story
of the Crucifixion, the greatest New Testament illustration
of God's passionate personality is seen in the parable of the
prodigal son. It contains one of the most comprehensive
descriptions of God's emotional makeup in Scripture.

In Luke 15:11–24 Jesus recounted the story:

> There was a man who had two sons. The younger one
> said to his father, "Father, give me my share of the
> estate." So he divided his property between them.
>
> Not long after that, the younger son got together
> all he had, set off for a distant country and there

squandered his wealth in wild living. After he had spent everything, there was a severe famine in that whole country, and he began to be in need. So he went and hired himself out to a citizen of that country, who sent him to his fields to feed pigs. He longed to fill his stomach with the pods that the pigs were eating, but no one gave him anything.

When he came to his senses, he said, "How many of my father's hired men have food to spare, and here I am starving to death! I will set out and go back to my father and say to him: Father, I have sinned against heaven and against you. I am no longer worthy to be called your son; make me like one of your hired men." So he got up and went to his father.

But while he was still a long way off, his father saw him and was filled with compassion for him; he ran to his son, threw his arms around him and kissed him.

The son said to him, "Father, I have sinned against heaven and against you. I am no longer worthy to be called your son."

But the father said to his servants, "Quick! Bring the best robe and put it on him. Put a ring on his finger and sandals on his feet. Bring the fattened calf and kill it. Let's have a feast and celebrate. For this son of mine was dead and is alive again; he was lost and is found." So they began to celebrate.

In the Jewish culture this never would have happened. For the younger son to demand his inheritance prior to his father's death would be equivalent to saying "I wish you were dead."

When the prodigal had spent all he had, he decided to return to his father. Even while he was off in the distance, the father saw him. The father had been looking for him.

He couldn't wait for his youngest son to come home. Look at the next thing the father did. He ran. He kissed him. He had compassion on him. He brought him home. He killed the fattened calf and put a ring on his son's finger. He even put a robe on his shoulders. Can you sense the passion of God's heart in the response of the father?

This story is really all about the father's heart. The younger son wasted his inheritance and became immoral; yet as he cried out for forgiveness, the father welcomed him with open arms. Yes, the prodigal had hit rock bottom. Yes, he was desperate. But he could have stayed where he was. Many prodigals do.

What gave the prodigal the courage to return home? I believe that during his childhood the prodigal saw something in his father that let him know he would not be rejected if he returned home. Although he knew he had made a tragic mistake, he had a realistic understanding of who his father was. It empowered him to return home and be restored.

For you to fully enjoy the Father, you need to have a deep understanding of His personality. If you are continually afraid of being rejected by Him and feel that He's perpetually angry with you because of things you've done, how can you open your heart to Him? How can you freely give yourself to Him and obey Him?

Like the prodigal son, some of you may be struggling with addictions or temptations, and the shame you carry may be overwhelming. You may have made numerous New Year's resolutions and tried different self-imposed disciplines. You may have even spent countless hours in counseling and deliverance ministry. Yet you're still wrestling with the power of temptation.

One of the strongest and most gripping of these, especially for men, is sexual temptation. If this is you, what you need to realize is that a lot of the energy that fuels sexual impurity comes from rejection and not rebellion. It may be rejection you experienced when you were growing up, or it may even be the misguided rejection you feel from God. Whatever the reason may be, you need to understand that immorality is a counterfeit intimacy. It's nothing more than a subtle form of escapism. It brings with it a false sense of fulfillment, and it tempts you to cover up your hopelessness and pain with something that will only bring you temporary pleasure at best.

The only thing that will ultimately break the power of lust in your life is a revelation of the Father's love. Like the prodigal son, you need to experience the running, embracing, kissing heart of God. The sweet fragrance of the Father's affections is the one thing that will deliver you from the seductive scent of sexual sin.

If you have a hard time identifying with the prodigal son, it may be because you've never been involved in "prodigal living." But I wonder how many of you can relate more readily to the elder brother. While the prodigal is usually the focus of most sermons, the elder brother is actually a very important part of the parable.

As we return to the story, we find that:

> The older son was in the field. When he came near the house, he heard music and dancing. So he called one of the servants and asked him what was going on. "Your brother has come," he replied, "and your father has killed the fattened calf because he has him back safe and sound."
>
> The older brother became angry and refused to go in. So his father went out and pleaded with him. But he answered his father, "Look! All these years I've been slaving for you and never disobeyed your orders.

> Yet you never gave me even a young goat so I could celebrate with my friends. But when this son of yours who has squandered your property with prostitutes comes home, you kill the fattened calf for him!"
>
> "My son," the father said, "you are always with me, and everything I have is yours. But we had to celebrate and be glad, because this brother of yours was dead and is alive again; he was lost and is found."
>
> —LUKE 15:25–32

Notice that the elder brother had remained in his father's house the whole time his younger brother was gone. Yet because he was so performance driven, he couldn't understand the father's response to his prodigal brother. There was something buried in his personality that made him feel as if he had to strive to earn his father's love.

Do you feel the same way toward your heavenly Father? Do you find yourself continually striving to win His favor? One reason people struggle with the unconditional love of the Father is unbalanced teaching about the nature of God's character. You may have sat under a ministry that emphasized the severity of God's judgment against sin at the expense of not underscoring the goodness of the Father's heart. This kind of teaching can contribute to various forms of legalism as well as an unhealthy view of God.

Legalism is an attempt to earn the Father's love through works rather than knowing His approval through the work of the cross. It causes you to base your relationship with God on personal discipline rather than on the sacrifice of Christ. It even causes good people to replace their love for God with a love for the things of God.

Another reason many of us try to earn the Father's love is that we're deeply aware of how much we have failed Him. We try to overcome our guilt and shame by showing Him how sincerely sorry we are. And through it all the Father is whispering to us, "I don't want your efforts. I want you. My love for you is a gift. You don't deserve it, and you can't earn it. I want to give it to you simply because you're Mine."

Years ago I read a story that parallels the parable of the prodigal son. It was about a young man by the name of Sawat:

> [He] had disgraced his family and dishonored his father's name. He had come to Bangkok to escape the dullness of village life. He had found excitement, and while he prospered in his sordid lifestyle he had found popularity as well.
>
> When he first arrived, he had visited a hotel unlike any he had ever seen. Every room had a window facing into the hallway, and in every room sat a girl. The older ones smiled and laughed. Others, just 12 or 13 years old or younger, looked nervous, even frightened.
>
> That visit began Sawat's venture into Bangkok's world of prostitution. It began innocently enough, but he was quickly caught like a small piece of wood in a raging river. Its force was too powerful and swift for him, the current too strong.
>
> Soon he was selling opium to customers and propositioning tourists in the hotels. He even went so low as to actually help buy and sell young girls, some of them only nine and ten years old. It was a nasty business, and he was one of the most important of the young "businessmen."
>
> Then the bottom dropped out of his world: He hit a string of bad luck. He was robbed, and while trying to climb back to the top, he was arrested. The word went out in the underworld that he was a police spy. He finally ended up living in a shanty by the city trash pile.
>
> Sitting in his little shack, he thought about his

family, especially his father, a simple Christian man from a small southern village near the Malaysian border. He remembered his dad's parting words: "I am waiting for you." He wondered whether his father would still be waiting for him after all that he had done to dishonor the family name. Would he be welcome in his home? Word of Sawat's lifestyle had long ago filtered back to the village.

Finally he devised a plan.

"Dear Father," he wrote, "I want to come home, but I don't know if you will receive me after all that I have done. I have sinned greatly, father. Please forgive me. On Saturday night I will be on the train that goes through our village. If you are still waiting for me, will you tie a piece of cloth on the po tree in front of our house? (Signed) Sawat."

On that train ride he reflected on his life over the past few months and knew that his father had every right to deny him. As the train finally neared the village, he churned with anxiety. What would he do if there was no white cloth on the po tree?

Sitting opposite him was a kind stranger who noticed how nervous his fellow passenger had become. Finally Sawat could stand the pressure no longer. He blurted out his story in a torrent of words. As they entered the village, Sawat said, "Oh, sir, I cannot bear to look. Can you watch for me? What if my father will not receive me back?"

Sawat buried his face between his knees. "Do you see it, sir? It's the only house with a po tree."

"Young man, your father did not hang just one piece of cloth. Look! He has covered the whole tree with cloth!" Sawat could hardly believe his eyes. The branches were laden with tiny white squares. In the front yard his old father jumped up and down, joyously waving a piece of white cloth, then ran in halting steps beside the train. When it stopped at the little station he threw his arms around his son, embracing him with tears of joy. "I've been waiting for you!" he exclaimed.[9]

FACING OUR PAST

Some of you may be thinking that if God is so affectionate, then why did He allow you to go through such a horrible past? Why did He allow you to be raised in a broken home? Why did He allow the abuse? Why did He allow the children in the schoolyard to taunt and torment you? Why did your loved one have to die? Why did He allow the pain? Why did He allow any of it?

These are deep questions for which I offer no pat answers. But I do know that the call of the divine romance will enable you to look beyond your pain and catch a glimpse of what God has gone through to bring you to Himself. Do you think you've gone through pain? No one has ever gone through the pain and suffering the Father went through to reveal Himself to you in a way that would bring fulfillment to your heart.

It's not my point to make light of anyone's experiences. There's definitely a place for counseling, nurturing, healing, and restoration. But if you will embrace the reality of God as your Father, your heart will be warmed to the truth that He can be trusted. Even what the devil has meant for your destruction your heavenly Father will eventually work for good. In other words, He will recycle your trash.

Everyone has a unique testimony and destiny. Regardless of the things you have gone through, your heavenly Father continually wants to bring redemption out of your pain and trauma. Some of you will be better able to relate to those who have gone through a divorce, grown up in a broken home, or lost a loved one. Others of you will touch a segment of humanity that many people will never be able to touch. You will know what those people have endured because you have gone through it yourself. The Father invites you to be healed of your past so you, in turn, can bring hope and healing to others. Out of your own unique journey you will be able to introduce others to the passionate heart of the Father.

The Approachable Father

If you have experienced the hard-nosed, hurtful, and sometimes even abusive actions of an authoritarian father, then you may still have difficulty opening your heart to the heavenly Father and resting in His love. Like a beaten puppy you find yourself withdrawing and shrinking from His authority, because you assume He will be just like the other authority figures in your life. You want to completely submit your life to Him, but you're afraid He will take advantage of you. But He won't.

You must realize that God is different from any other authority figure you've ever known. He isn't perpetually angry with you. He isn't just tolerating you. He enjoys you, even in your weakness and immaturity.

The Father has blessed me with two sons. When they were babies, they couldn't communicate with me. They couldn't play golf with me. They couldn't do anything but eat, sleep, and make messes. But I loved them intensely! Even when they started growing and maturing, I still didn't love them any more than I did when they were babies. They were just in a different season of their lives.

First John 4:15–18 says, "If anyone acknowledges that Jesus is the Son of God, God lives in him and he in God. And so we know and rely on the love God has for us. God is love. Whoever lives in love lives in God, and God in him. In this way, love is made complete among us so that we will have confidence on the day of judgment, because in this world we are like him. There is no fear in love. But perfect love drives out fear, because fear has to do with punishment. The one who fears is not made perfect in love."

Do you get the message? God is not an authoritarian Father. He doesn't want you shrinking back in fear or apprehension of Him. He's an approachable Father who loves you passionately.

In *God in Search of Man,* Abraham Joshua Heschel explains that the phrase "the fear of God" is derived from the Hebrew word *yirah.* He writes:

> The word has two meanings—fear and awe. There is the man who fears the Lord lest he be punished in his body, family, or in his possessions. Another man fears the Lord because he is afraid of punishment in the life to come. Both types are considered inferior in Jewish tradition. Job, who said, "Though he slay me, yet will I trust in Him" (Job 13:15), was not motivated by fear but rather by awe, by the realization of the grandeur of eternal love.
>
> Fear is the anticipation of evil or pain, as contrasted with hope which is the anticipation of good. Awe, on the other hand, is the sense of wonder and humility inspired by the sublime or felt in the presence of mystery....Awe, unlike fear, does not make us shrink from the awe-inspiring object, but, on the contrary, draws us near to it. This is why awe is compatible with both love and joy. In a very real sense, awe is the antithesis of fear. To feel "The Lord is my light and my salvation" is to feel "Whom shall I fear?" (Ps. 27:1). "God is our refuge and strength. A very present help in trouble. Therefore we will not fear, even though the earth be removed, and though the mountains be carried into the midst of the sea" (Ps. 46:1–2).[10]

111

The fear of the Lord is not a tormenting, demonic fear. It's not an emotional fear or even a fear of God's wrath. Proverbs 8:13 says, "To fear the Lord is to hate evil." Being in awe of God simply means that you love Him so much that you hate what He hates. You hate the destructiveness of sin. You hate anything that has the potential to hurt your heavenly Father.

It is the awe and fascination of the Father that bring us close to His heart and lead us into a life of spiritual and emotional wholeness. Proverbs 14:26 tells us, "In the fear of the LORD there is strong confidence" (NKJV). We can rest assured that even when He disciplines and corrects us, He still enjoys us. Far too many Christians mistake divine correction for rejection. But the Father's correction is deeply rooted in His affection for us. Proverbs 3:11–12 admonishes us to "not despise the LORD's discipline and do not resent his rebuke, because the LORD disciplines those he loves, as a father the son he delights in." While He may be displeased with a certain area in our lives, He is not displeased with us as a person.

We can see this portrayed in the lives of the disciples. During the time surrounding the Last Supper (John 13–17), Jesus began preparing them for the disappointments, temptations, and persecution they would face. How did He do it? By repeatedly speaking of the Father's loving desire for them (John 17:23, 26). Even though He knew they would all deeply hurt Him by abandoning Him in His darkest hour of need (Matt. 26:31), He never gave up on them. He saw the sincerity of their hearts. Although they were immature, they were not rebels. In fact, Jesus made an interesting statement in John 13:10. He looked at His disciples and said, "And you are clean, though not every one of you." He was referring to Judas when He spoke of the one exception.

Judas was unclean because he had a heart of betrayal. In contrast, Jesus told the other eleven disciples that they were clean. How could they be considered clean and still be spiritually immature? Because immaturity is not the same thing as rebellion.

It's imperative that we understand that the Father deals with us according to the sincerity of our hearts. Although He sees the undeveloped areas of our character, He also hears the willing cry of our spirits. As we set our hearts on obeying Him, He will make loving adjustments in our lives until we come to maturity.

Over the years far too many ministers have taken passages that clearly referred to the rebellious and have tried to make them applicable to sincere, immature believers. They've attempted to scare the immature into maturity. But this simply doesn't work. The fruit doesn't last.

We see this principle clearly demonstrated in the life of Peter. Although Peter never dreamed he would deny the Lord three times, Jesus had clearly warned him it would happen. While Peter had a willing heart to serve the Lord, he never realized how weak and immature he actually was (Matt. 26:41). When he came face-to-face with what he had done and with the weakness of his own flesh, the shame was too much for him to bear. He decided to return to fishing, because that was the only thing he knew to do. What else could he have done? He had given up on any chance of future ministry, and he had even given up on himself.

But the Lord had not given up on Peter, and, in reality, Peter hadn't given up on the Lord. According to John 21:7, when Peter heard that Jesus was standing on the seashore watching him fish, he immediately jumped into the water and swam to Him. Someone with a heart of betrayal would not have done that.

Can you imagine what took place between the two of them as their eyes met? I can picture Peter falling into the arms of Jesus and sobbing uncontrollably as the Lord embraced him and forgave him. What a moment that must have been!

Before we leave the story, I want you to notice how Jesus broke the shame from Peter's life. Just as Peter had denied the Lord three times, Jesus asked Peter the same question three times—"Do you love Me?" Now it should be obvious that when the Lord asked Peter these questions, it wasn't because He was "fishing" for information (pun intended). According to John 21:17, and specifically the phrase, "Lord, you know all things," it's clear that Jesus was up to something. He knew that Peter loved Him. He saw the sincerity of his heart and understood that Peter wanted to serve Him.

When Jesus asked Peter three times if he loved Him, He was not trying to get even with Peter for denying Him three times. He was calling Peter back to an intimate relationship. Jesus wanted Peter to say "I love You" so that every time those words were spoken, Peter would be gripped by their power and would allow them to melt the shame from his life.

TRANSPARENT BEFORE THE FATHER

Once you begin to understand the depths of God's love for you and the nature of His heart, then you will be able to be transparent with Him. Intimacy requires communication, vulnerability, and honesty. Maybe you had to hide things from your earthly father due to fear and intimidation. But you certainly don't need to hide anything from your heavenly Father. Besides, you can't anyway, so you might as well quit trying.

Like Peter, you may still be carrying the shame of your

past failures and may be having a hard time forgiving yourself. You may have even become accustomed to a second-class relationship with the Lord because you're afraid you might fail again. Because you think the Father is angry and exasperated with you, you run from Him instead of running to Him. It's not that you don't love Him; it's just that you're living under the weight of guilt and condemnation. But the Father sees the sincerity of your heart, and He wants you to be real with Him. He wants you to open your heart to Him. Don't shrink back. You're not going to make Him blush. He is waiting with open arms to restore you, but He can't do that if you are living in denial or are afraid to come to Him. In your times of confession, get real with your Father. Be completely honest. You can trust Him. He fully understands what you're going through. And He will wash away your shame.

CLOSING PRAYER

Father, You have promised to never leave me. Forgive me for believing at times that You were absent in my life. Thank You for making me Your child and friend. I ask that You deepen our relationship and help me to understand the depths of Your love, acceptance, and compassion. I need to know how You see me. Reveal Yourself and Your vision for my life. Help me to see what You see and recognize Your involvement in my life. Continue renewing me until I am wholly Yours. In Jesus's name.

God made man to experience the satisfying pleasures of His presence instead of the temporary pleasures of sin.

love-empowered holiness

chapter 7

The story is told of a desert nomad who awoke one night with an insatiable appetite. The nomad lit a candle and looked around his tent for something to eat. His eyes eventually focused on a bag of dates propped up in a corner. Being extremely hungry, he reached into the bag and pulled out a date. He took one bite and spit it out. Inside the date he discovered a worm. But he was so hungry that he reached back into the bag, grabbed another date, and proceeded to bite into another worm. He even tried a third date, but all he got was a mouthful of worm. You would have thought he'd stop eating; instead he blew out the candle and in the darkness of his tent ate the entire bag of dates.

Within every human being there's an insatiable appetite for happiness and fulfillment. The desire is so strong that at times people will blow out the candle of their conscience, regardless of the "worms" or the consequences of their sin. Even though they know better, they choose to suffer the consequences just to experience a passing moment of pleasure.

The great American theologian Jonathan Edwards understood this universal longing for happiness inherent in every man and woman. He once said:

> They certainly are the wisest men that do those things
> that make most for their happiness, and this in effect

is acknowledged by all men in the world, for there is no man upon the earth who isn't earnestly seeking after happiness, and it appears abundantly by the variety of ways they so vigorously seek it; they will twist and turn every way...to make themselves happy men. Some will wander all over the face of the earth to find it: they will seek it in the waters and dry land, under the waters and in the bowels of the earth, and although the true way to happiness lies right before them and they might easily step into it and walk in it and be brought into as great a happiness as they desire, and greater than they can conceive of, yet they will not enter into it. They try all the false paths; they will spend and be spent...endanger their lives, will pass over mountains and valleys, go through fire and water, seeking for happiness amongst vanities, and are always disappointed, never find what they seek for; but yet like fools and madmen they violently rush forward, still in the same ways. But the righteous are not so; these only have the wisdom to find the right paths to happiness.[1]

It's disturbing to me that Christians have been taught to suppress their deepest desires for pleasure and happiness. Over the years I've heard ministers emphatically declare, "God isn't interested in whether or not we're happy. All He cares about is that we glorify and serve Him." I would agree that God's glory should be the primary focus of our lives. But I would strongly suggest that God is most glorified in us when we are most satisfied in Him. In other words, the greatest way we can glorify the Father is by enjoying Him and finding our ultimate happiness in Him.

Some of us may be uncomfortable using the word *happiness* in relation to Christian service. To serve God for our own happiness and satisfaction appears to be selfish, to say the least. We tend to measure the value of an act of service by the amount of pain and sacrifice that's required. Doing something simply for enjoyment seems to devalue the act.

In reality, we always choose what we think will ultimately give us the greatest happiness and pleasure. Even if we make decisions that are painful and costly to us, we believe that such choices will produce the greatest fulfillment in the long run.

Hebrews 11:24–26 tells us, "By faith Moses, when he had grown up, refused to be known as the son of Pharaoh's daughter. He chose to be mistreated along with the people of God rather than to enjoy the pleasures of sin for a short time. He regarded disgrace for the sake of Christ as of greater value than the treasures of Egypt, because he was looking ahead to his reward."

Moses found himself captivated by a greater pleasure. He discovered the happiness that obedience can bring. Moses looked beyond the temporary pleasures of sin and embraced the eternal rewards that would one day be his. In other words, he believed that the long-term benefits of obedience far outweighed the short-term benefits of living in Pharaoh's palace.

God made man to experience the satisfying pleasures of His presence instead of the temporary pleasures of sin. Jesus continually appealed to man's innate desire for lasting happiness and fulfillment by speaking of eternal rewards and using them as incentives for choosing the kingdom of His Father.

Consider the Beatitudes. In Matthew 5:3–12 Jesus taught key principles for kingdom living and offered a series of rewards for those who would obey them. Look very closely at the language of these verses: "Blessed are the poor in spirit, for theirs is the kingdom of heaven. Blessed are those who mourn, for they will be comforted. Blessed are the meek, for they will inherit the earth. Blessed are those who hunger and thirst for righteousness, for they will be filled. Blessed are the merciful, for they will be shown mercy. Blessed are the pure in heart, for they will see God. Blessed are the peacemakers, for they will be called sons of God. Blessed are those who are persecuted because of righteousness, for theirs is the kingdom of heaven" (vv. 3–10).

Get the message? The alternative to the temporary pleasures of the kingdom of this world is the permanent pleasures of the Father's kingdom. Jesus never calls us to a life of religious misery. He never compels us to do anything out of religious duty. He invites us instead to experience the pleasures of His heart and the satisfaction of obeying Him.

Attempting to perform our Christian duties without delighting in our Father is really an insult to Him. Although we have a responsibility to obey His Word and do His will, if our motivation for doing so is merely duty and not the delight that comes as a reward for obedience, our Father is not honored.

As I mentioned in a previous chapter, my wife and I have been married for more than forty years. To celebrate our anniversary, I often take her to one of her favorite restaurants and give her a dozen long-stemmed roses. What would her reaction be if, after she thanked me for the great meal and the lovely flowers, I simply said, "There's no need to thank me. I'm just doing my duty as a husband"? I doubt that my anniversary would be a happy occasion.

On the other hand, if I took her to the restaurant, gave her the flowers, and then told her that being with her was more important to me than anything in the world, I would not only be expressing my love for her, but I would also be honoring her as my wife.

Likewise, if I want to honor and glorify my Father as well as express my deepest devotion to Him, the best thing I can do is enjoy Him and derive my greatest pleasure from Him.

In Psalm 16:11 David explained why he continually longed for God: "You have made known to me the path of life; you will fill me with joy in your presence, with eternal pleasures at your right hand." Think about it! What an incentive for loving the Father with all our hearts! We are being offered a joy and pleasure that surpass any human experience. And the only place these things can truly be found is in the Father's presence.

No human relationship can ultimately satisfy us. Taking drugs can't do it. Getting drunk can't do it. Illicit sex can't do it. Money can't even buy it. Only knowing and experiencing the Father can give us the happiness and pleasure that our hearts so desperately crave.

Throughout His Word the Father continually appeals to our desire for happiness and fulfillment (Pss. 34:8, 36:8, 43:4, 63:3, 119:103; Jer. 29:13; Matt. 13:44). He does so because He has placed within each of us an unrelenting appetite for satisfaction and pleasure. Our desire for such things will never let up.

As Christians we have an obligation to be as happy as we possibly can. Pursuing pleasure is not optional; it is even commanded, "Delight yourself in the LORD and he will give you the desires of your heart" (Ps. 37:4). Our longing for happiness was the Father's intent for us from the beginning, so we would learn to find our fulfillment and pleasure in Him.

In his book *The Weight of Glory*, C. S. Lewis wrote this:

> If you asked twenty good men today what they thought the highest of the virtues, nineteen of them would reply, Unselfishness. But if you asked almost

any of the great Christians of old he would have replied, Love. You see what has happened? A negative term has been substituted for a positive, and this is of more than philological importance. The negative idea of Unselfishness carries with it the suggestion not primarily of securing good things for others, but of going without them ourselves, as if our abstinence and not their happiness was the important point. I do not think this is the Christian virtue of Love.

The New Testament has lots to say about self-denial, but not self-denial as an end in itself. We are told to deny ourselves and to take up our crosses in order that we may follow Christ; and nearly every description of what we shall ultimately find if we do so contains an appeal to desire. If there lurks in most modern minds the notion that to desire our own good and earnestly to hope for it is a bad thing, I submit that this notion has crept in from Kant and the Stoics and is no part of the Christian faith. Indeed, if we consider the unblushing promises of reward and the staggering nature of the rewards promised in the Gospels, it would seem that our Lord finds our desires not too strong, but too weak. We are half-hearted creatures, fooling about with drink and sex and ambition when infinite joy is offered us, like an ignorant child who wants to go on making mud pies in a slum because he cannot imagine what is meant by the offer of a holiday at the sea. We are far too easily pleased.[2]

One of the most damaging ideas the church has promoted is the notion that the desire for happiness and pleasure is evil. The belief that holiness and happiness are at odds with each other is a serious twisting of Christian truth. We are told to either crucify our desires for happiness and pleasure or pretend that these desires don't exist within our hearts. No wonder so many Christians are both bored and overwhelmed with condemnation. On the one hand, our hearts long to be fascinated by something; on the other hand, we feel guilty because we still have the desire for pleasure and fulfillment.

The truth is that there is no contradiction between holiness and happiness. In fact, holiness can best be attained by finding our ultimate happiness and pleasure in God.

Why do people sin? They sin because they enjoy the pleasure that it brings. Hebrews 11:25 speaks of the temporary pleasures of sin. No one sins out of duty. People sin because they believe the pleasure it brings is more satisfying than the pleasure obedience brings. Or as someone once said, "Sin is what you do when your heart is not satisfied with God."[3]

In this chapter I'm looking at the subject of holiness from a somewhat unique perspective. The traditional approach to discouraging people from sinning is negative. The church has often tried to use threats and warnings as deterrents to sinful living. Christian leaders have attempted to scare sincere but immature believers into maturity.

However, this simply doesn't work. I'm not suggesting there's no place for warnings, but if a man's heart is not being warmed by the passions of God's personality, his heart will be captivated by the red-hot flames of temptation. It doesn't matter how much he's challenged or threatened. If a man who is susceptible to the lure of pornography is sitting in a hotel room and has the opportunity to rent an X-rated movie, warnings alone will often do no good. His heart has to be captured by something more satisfying.

Years ago the First Lady of the United States challenged the youth of America to "Just Say *No*" to drugs as she warned them of the dangers of drug use. When I first heard the expression, I thought, "Does she really believe that this is all it's going to take to solve our drug problem?" However, in thinking about it further, I realized that this is the same kind of strategy the church has used for years to try to keep people from sinning. We've told them to "Just Say No" to illicit sex or getting drunk or some other vice. But just saying no alone doesn't work. There must be something more appealing to which a person can say yes. A person must experience something that will offer him a greater pleasure than the allurements of sin.

People buy into the false premise that sin will make them happier than God can. Even though this is a lie, how many individuals honestly believe that obedience will bring a greater pleasure in their lives than sin ever could? If they really believed it, they wouldn't want to sin. Getting drunk or high on drugs are just counterfeits for what people could experience in God's presence.

Yet people settle for far too little pleasure. They go after other lovers and lesser joys that can only give them momentary satisfaction. The things that quickly thrill them just as quickly disappoint them. They discover all too late that they've become entangled in a web of destructive behavior.

Ultimately the only thing that will liberate the human heart from the slavery of sin is the supreme satisfaction found in God. I believe many Christians have made the mistake of attempting to discourage people from sinning by only exposing the ugliness of the world and its ways.

Even the message of holiness is often relegated to nothing more than a list of forbidden activities. Because of my denominational background, if you had mentioned the word *holiness* to me years ago, it would have dialed up a number of negative reactions and emotions. I would have had visions of women with no makeup, men with no wedding bands or jewelry of any kind, and young women playing softball in dresses because they weren't allowed to wear slacks.

Yet holiness will never be attained by following man-made rules and regulations. Rules and regulations don't have the ability to thrill the human heart. They are bland and lifeless. I have known people who appeared to do everything "right" externally but later fell apart spiritually because their motivation for obedience to the Word wasn't based on an intimate love relationship with the One they were outwardly serving.

Most people can be motivated only so long by willpower, determination, hype, or fear. Eventually the trials and temptations of life will either cause them to go deeper in their intimacy with the Father or reveal that they are only serving Him superficially. The motivation for their service is not based on a close relationship with Him.

Holiness can only be truly experienced as we embrace God's promise of supreme happiness and pleasure. This is the heart of the message of holiness. The pure in heart *will* see God (Matt. 5:8). The pure in heart will get to experience and enjoy Him.

THE TRANSFORMING POWER OF BEAUTY

There is something intriguing about God! The psalmist David understood this in a way very few men ever have. No wonder he wrote in Psalm 27:4, "One thing I ask of the Lord, this is what I seek: that I may dwell in the house of the Lord all the days of my life, to gaze upon the beauty of the Lord and to seek him in his temple."

Beauty isn't a word we normally associate with God. Yet it's the word David used on more than one occasion to speak of God's character and personality. There is perhaps no better way to enjoy God than to see Him for who He really is. The more we meditate on the Scriptures, take to heart the breathtaking truths about God, and allow them to saturate our minds and emotions, the more we'll become fascinated by His beauty.

God alone is beautiful in an absolute sense. He is infinitely splendid. He is glorious in majesty, and His grandeur is incomprehensible. He has put Himself on display in the art gallery of the universe and invited us to bask in His beauty and enjoy Him to the fullest.

This is what we were made for—to enjoy God and the greatness of who He is. In fact, God personally invites us to seek His face and behold His beauty. In Psalm 27:8 we read, "When You said, 'Seek My face,' My heart said to You, 'Your face, LORD, I will seek'" (NKJV).

God doesn't want just the works of our hands. He wants us to behold His face. David even suggested that we're to worship the Lord in the "beauty of holiness" (1 Chron. 16:29, NKJV), a phrase that refers to the beauty of who God is. God is holy. In other words, God is beautiful. He's the antithesis of sin and evil. He's perfectly pure. He's unique and distinct from all others. He's a unique "Father." He's a unique "lover." And He calls us to love Him and experience Him.

Beholding the beauty of the Lord is invigorating and enjoyable. It's also deeply transforming. This is what the apostle Paul was referring to in 2 Corinthians 3:18: "But we all, with unveiled face, beholding as in a mirror the glory of the Lord, are being transformed into the same image from glory to glory" (NKJV). In other words, to behold Him is to be like Him. The more we meditate on the perfection and passions of God's character and personality, the more we'll become like our Father.

One of the reasons so many professions of faith miscarry is that while we call people to make decisions for Christ, we bring them to a point of crisis without further leading them to a place of contemplation. The conversions that last are based on a "beholding as in a mirror the glory of the Lord." What captures the human heart is the unsurpassing value of Jesus!

This is what holiness is all about. Holiness isn't about rules and regulations; it's about getting carried away into a passionate relationship with God. People can adhere to certain external requirements and still not be holy. Power for holy living flows from a relationship with the Holy One. In Exodus 3:5 the ground was holy because God was there. The more we experience the One who lives in us, the holier we'll become. The power of the Father's presence imparts purity.

This is why I believe we can't break the power of sin in our lives by just saying no to temptation. Saying no is critical, but that's not all that's required. If it were, people would be able to keep all their New Year's resolutions, stay out of debt, and never have to diet again. Let's face it. Saying no isn't enough. The human heart has to be able to say yes to something better—namely, *Someone* better.

The affection for lesser lovers must be replaced by a greater affection. And that's where love-empowered holiness comes in. Overcoming sin is not about gritting your teeth and holding on for dear life. The only way for you to successfully resist sin is by maximizing your pleasure in God. The Father wants you to be a glutton for His presence. He wants you to become addicted to Him. He wants your heart to be seized by the matchless value and delight of His being.

THE JOY OF THE TREASURE

Brennan Manning shares the following story in his book *Abba's Child*:

> It appears to be just another long day of manual labor in the weary rhythm of time. But suddenly the ox stops and tugs mischievously. The peasant drives his

plowshare deeper into the earth than he usually does. He turns over furrow after furrow until he hears the sound of a harsh metallic noise. The ox stops pawing. The man pushes the primitive plow aside.

With his bare hands he furiously digs up the earth. The dirt flies everywhere. At last the peasant spies a handle and lifts a large earthen pot out of the ground. Trembling, he yanks the handle off the pot. He is stunned. He lets out a scream—"Yaaaahh!"—that makes the ox blink.

The heavy pot is filled to the rim with coins and jewels, silver, and gold. He rifles through the treasure, letting the precious coins, the rare earrings, and sparkling diamonds slip through his fingers. Furtively, the peasant looks around to see if anyone has been watching him. Satisfied that he is alone, he heaps the dirt over the earthen pot, plows a shallow furrow over the surface, lays a large stone at the spot as a marker and resumes plowing the field.

He is deeply affected by his splendid find. A single thought absorbs him; in fact, it so controls him that he can no longer work undistracted by day or sleep undisturbed by night.

The field must become his property!

As a day laborer it is impossible for him to take possession of the buried treasure. Where can he get the money to buy the field? Caution and discretion fly out the window. He sells everything he owns. He gets a fair price for his hut and the few sheep he has acquired. He turns to relatives, friends, and acquaintances and borrows significant sums. The owner of the field is delighted with the fancy price offered by the purchaser and sells to the peasant without a second thought.

The new owner's wife is apoplectic. His sons are inconsolable. His friends reproach him. His neighbors wag their heads: "He stayed out too long in the sun." Still, they are baffled by his prodigious energy.

The peasant remains unruffled, even joyful, in the face of widespread opposition. He knows he has stumbled on an extraordinarily profitable transaction and rejoices at the thought of the payoff. The treasure, which apparently had been buried in the field for security before the last war and whose owner had not survived, returns a hundredfold on the price he had paid. He pays off all his debts and builds the equivalent of a mansion in Malibu. The lowly peasant is now a man whose fortune is made, envied by his enemies, congratulated by his friends, and secure for the rest of his life.[4]

In Matthew 13:44, Jesus said, "The kingdom of heaven is like treasure hidden in a field, which a man found and hid; and for joy over it he goes and sells all that he has and buys that field" (NKJV). Notice the phrase "and for joy over it." It was the joy of discovering the treasure that motivated the man to sell everything he had. And it's the discovery of the incomparable value and delight of the treasure—Jesus—that enables an individual to give up everything for the sake of the kingdom.

Commenting on this parable, Joachim Jeremias observed:

> When that great joy surpassing all measure seizes a man, it carries him away, penetrates his inmost being, subjugates his mind. All else seems valueless compared to that surpassing worth. No price is too great to pay. The unreserved surrender of what is most valuable becomes a matter of course. The decisive thing in the parable is not what the man gives up, but his reason for doing so—the overwhelming experience of their discovery. Thus it is with the Kingdom of God. The

effect of the joyful news is overpowering; it fills the heart with gladness; it changes the whole direction of one's life and produces the most wholehearted self-sacrifice.[5]

This should be the true motivation for radical commitment—getting caught up in the joy of the treasure. This is what propelled many of the great men and women of God throughout history to live and die for the kingdom of God. Although David Livingstone, Hudson Taylor, and other pioneer missionaries gave up everything for the gospel, they didn't consider it a sacrifice, because they were fascinated by the treasure.

It was the overwhelming joy and delight of "discovering" the treasure that motivated Mary to lavishly give of the treasure of her life to Jesus (Mark 14:3–9). It wasn't a sacrifice for her; she had experienced the forgiveness and unconditional love of her Savior. Her heart had been captivated by a priceless treasure. Although the disciples were embarrassed and put off by her actions, Jesus was so moved by what she did that He made it an eternal monument of extravagant love (v. 9).

When we truly experience the joy of our treasure, we will also get carried away and lost in His love. No price will be considered too great to pay as we gaze on the unrivaled worth and value of the lover of our hearts.

Martyred missionary Jim Elliot once said, "A man is no fool to give up what he cannot keep to gain what he cannot lose." This was at the heart of what Jesus said in Mark 8:34–35: "If anyone would come after me, he must deny himself and take up his cross and follow me. For whoever wants to save his life will lose it, but whoever loses his life for me and for the gospel will save it." Jesus wants us to deny ourselves the lesser joys of this life so we won't lose the bigger ones in the life to come. He doesn't want us settling for anything less than the joy of the treasure of His heart.

Consider the example of Esau mentioned in Hebrews 12:15–17. We are challenged to, "See to it that no one misses the grace of God and that no bitter root grows up to cause trouble and defile many. See that no one is sexually immoral, or is godless like Esau, who for a single meal sold his inheritance rights as the oldest son. Afterward, as you know, when he wanted to inherit this blessing, he was rejected. He could bring about no change of mind, though he sought the blessing with tears."

Esau lost his inheritance because he chose a single meal instead of the blessings of his birthright. This is a graphic picture of those who refuse to deny themselves the temporary pleasures of sin and, in turn, miss the lasting pleasures and blessings found only in God. Esau's sin was not in choosing a meal but in despising his birthright.

Denying self is never a virtue in itself. A denial of self that is not based on the greater goal of enjoying God will simply become a seedbed for pride and legalism.

In Romans 3:23 Paul wrote, "For all have sinned and fall short of the glory of God." What did he mean by "falling short" of the glory of God? The best explanation is found in Romans 1:21–23: "For although they knew God, they neither glorified him as God nor gave thanks to him, but their thinking became futile and their foolish hearts were darkened. Although they claimed to be wise, they became fools and exchanged the glory of the immortal God for images…" The way we "fall short" of the glory of God is to exchange it for something of lesser value. All sin stems from failing to place supreme value on the glory and goodness of God. We exchange a priceless treasure for the trinkets of this world.

AFFECTION-BASED OBEDIENCE

Jesus wants a lovesick bride who will cherish Him above everything else. Lovesick people will endure anything and go anywhere for love (Song of Sol. 8:7). Cost is never the ultimate issue.

When the bride in the Song of Solomon understood that the bridegroom's love for her was better than the wine of this world, she abandoned herself to him. The exhilarating things of this world—even the good things—couldn't compare to the wine of his love. It was the revelation of his love and affection for her that released in her an extravagant obedience.

The revelation of the Lord's love and His enjoyment of our lives will also awaken in us the ability to love and enjoy Him. The more we enjoy Him, the easier it will be to obey Him. Obedience that is born out of the revelation of His deep affection for us always produces the strongest commitment.

By contrast, many Christian leaders have attempted to use fear and shame as a motivation for obedience. As a result, a number of believers have lived with a silent dread, believing that a day is coming when God was going to have one last chance to expose all of their faults, weaknesses, and struggles.

Passages such as 1 Corinthians 3:10–15 have been used to try to provoke individuals to radical obedience. However, what's overlooked is John's statement in 1 John 4:16–18: "And so we know and rely on the love God has for us. God is love. Whoever lives in love lives in God, and God in him. In this way, love is made complete among us so that we will have confidence on the day of judgment, because in this world we are like him. There is no fear in love. But perfect love drives out fear, because fear has to do with punishment. The man who fears has not been made perfect in love."

While the Scriptures clearly state that the works of the

believer will be tested by fire, Christians will never experience the fire of God's wrath. The fire that will test your works will be the fire of His love. Peter confirmed this by revealing the true motivation of the Father for having our faith and works tested. He stated that the purpose of the test is so "that the genuineness of your faith, being much more precious than gold that perishes, though it is tested by fire, may be found to praise, honor, and glory at the revelation of Jesus Christ" (1 Pet. 1:7, NKJV).

The Father's motive for testing your works will be positive, not negative. This is confirmed by the fact that the Greek word for "test" in verse 7 is the same word used in 1 Corinthians 3:13. This Greek word means "to test for approval." In other words, your Father will look for ways to approve your efforts and reward you.

He will reward you for every act of kindness and obedience, especially those hidden from the eyes of others (Matt. 6:1–6; 25:35–40). Even small acts, such as giving a cup of cold water to someone, will not go unnoticed by the Lord (Matt. 10:42). This explains how a housewife and mother can experience the same degree of reward as a well-known evangelist who has ministered to hundreds of thousands of people. The issue will not be the sphere of one's influence but the faithfulness of one's heart. Those who are given more talents will not be rewarded above the person with just one talent. Again, every individual will be rewarded according to his degree of faithfulness concerning what the Father called him to do. But in everything the Father's desire is that your works will be to the praise, honor, and glory of His Son—your Savior—Jesus Christ.

> So when we say, with the writer of Hebrews, that "it is appointed for mortals to die once, and after that the judgment," we are not saying, "and after that

133

the condemnation" (Heb. 9:27). We are saying, with John, that to "see God," to be in God's unspeakable light, will purge us of all darkness.[6]

Satan's goal is to make you afraid that God will reject you one day. This fear will always produce torment in your relationship with the Father. The fear of judgment will cause you to guard your heart from Him, and you will never be fully open to Him.

Loving and worshiping the Father without a guarded heart is vital for spiritual growth. When you understand that His personality is delightful to experience and His commandments are not burdensome but wholesome (Matt. 11:30; 1 John 5:3), you'll then want to freely give yourself to Him because you're in awe of Him.

Some may disagree with my approach to holiness because they believe that without strict guidelines, clear-cut boundaries, and a list of dos and don'ts, people will see how close they can get to sin without going overboard. There will always be those who will abuse grace and twist the true meaning of its message. I am far more concerned that people will end up being consumed by religious rules and regulations, lose touch with their hearts, and never really come to know the Father.

I believe that people who fall in love with the Father and have a revelation of His grace will not want to live in sin. Because they have experienced the joy of the treasure, they'll want to forsake lesser lovers for the supreme lover of their hearts. They won't want to hurt or grieve Him (Ps. 51:4). Even in our natural relationships, we don't want to do things that would hurt or disappoint the ones we love. Our motivation for pleasing them is our love for them, just as our love for our heavenly Father should be the motivation for pleasing Him.

I believe that when the church becomes lovesick through a revelation of the Father's love, we will see the church emerge in all the power and glory God intended it to have. Believers will be brought out of their boredom and lukewarmness and awakened to fervency and radical commitment.

The Keeping Power of Grace

Love-empowered holiness is also experienced in our lives as we learn to embrace the power of the Spirit in our attempts at serving God. Far too many of us try to serve Him solely on the basis of the strength of our wills. But all too often we have failed. We have been blinded to the awesome truth that Paul expressed in Romans 11:36: "For from him and through him and to him are all things." In other words, even our ability to serve Him comes from Him.

Our zeal for Him is really His work in us. Philippians 2:13 says, "For it is God who works in you to will and to act according to his good purpose." The very desire in our hearts to love and obey Him was placed there by the Father in the first place.

Legalism teaches us that our commitment to God motivates Him to be committed to us. On the other hand, the grace of God teaches us that His commitment to us is what enables us to be committed to Him. It's the romance of the gospel and the Father's commitment to us that release us from religious pride and legalism.

There is a way of "serving" the Father that belittles Him and robs Him of His glory. We have to be careful not to serve Him in a way that implies a deficiency on His part. The Father is not in need of our service or help. His purposes on earth are not sustained by our energy. We can add nothing of value to His kingdom that is not already His by right. Acts 17:24–25 says, "The God who made the world and everything in it is the Lord of heaven and earth and does not live in temples built by hands. And he is not served by human hands, as if he needed anything, because he himself gives all men life and breath and everything else."

In her book *Ministering to the Lord* Roxanne Brandt writes:

> How wrong the Church has been to teach new Christians that we are saved to serve God. No! We are saved primarily because He wants us for Himself. That is why He has "loved back my life from the pit of corruption and nothingness," and "cast all my sins behind [His] back" (Isa. 38:17, AMP). God isn't in the business of saving people because He needs servants to win the world for Christ, or because without us He might lose the battle against the devil. Yet many Christians believe that they are working for a semi-impotent God who needs their help and expects them to repay Him.
>
> The Bible never once tells us to do anything *for* God. It tells us that in His love and grace, God chose to *involve* us in what He was doing. We can work with Him and allow Him to work through us. Think of it![7]

The Father gives us the privilege of partnering with Him. He is not glorified by zealous recruits who want to help Him out. He is so completely self-sufficient and so overflowing in power that He glorifies Himself by providing all of His resources to help strengthen us, support us, and provide for all our needs as we seek to obey Him with all our hearts.

This principle is found throughout the Scriptures. As you meditate on the following passages, allow them to grip your heart. For example, look at all the "I wills" of the Father mentioned in the first passage.

136

I will surely gather them from all the lands where I banish them in my furious anger and great wrath; I will bring them back to this place and let them live in safety. They will be my people, and I will be their God. I will give them singleness of heart and action, so that they will always fear me for their own good and the good of their children after them. I will make an everlasting covenant with them: I will never stop doing good to them, and I will inspire them to fear me, so that they will never turn away from me. I will rejoice in doing them good and will assuredly plant them in this land with all my heart and soul.

—JEREMIAH 32:37–41

Since ancient times no one has heard, no ear has perceived, no eye has seen any God besides you, who acts on behalf of those who wait for him.

—ISAIAH 64:4

For the eyes of the LORD range throughout the earth to strengthen those whose hearts are fully committed to him.

—2 CHRONICLES 16:9

I am the vine; you are the branches. If a man remains in me and I in him, he will bear much fruit; apart from me you can do nothing.

—JOHN 15:5

No temptation has seized you except what is common to man. And God is faithful; he will not let you be tempted beyond what you can bear. But when you are tempted, he will also provide a way out so that you can stand up under it.

—I CORINTHIANS 10:13

But by the grace of God I am what I am, and his grace to me was not without effect. No, I worked harder than all of them—yet not I, but the grace of God that was with me.

—1 CORINTHIANS 15:10

Being confident of this, that he who began a good work in you will carry it on to completion until the day of Christ Jesus.

—PHILIPPIANS 1:6

With this in mind, we constantly pray for you, that our God may count you worthy of his calling, and that by his power he may fulfill every good purpose of yours and every act prompted by your faith. We pray this so that the name of our Lord Jesus may be glorified in you, and you in him, according to the grace of our God and the Lord Jesus Christ.

—2 THESSALONIANS 1:11–12

May the God of peace, who through the blood of the eternal covenant brought back from the dead our Lord Jesus, that great Shepherd of the sheep, equip you with everything good for doing his will, and may he work in us what is pleasing to him, through Jesus Christ, to whom be glory for ever and ever. Amen.

—HEBREWS 13:20–21

If anyone speaks, he should do it as one speaking the very words of God. If anyone serves, he should do it with the strength God provides, so that in all things God may be praised through Jesus Christ. To him be the glory and the power for ever and ever. Amen.

—1 PETER 4:11

The radical call to holiness and discipleship isn't just a call to serve Jesus. It's a call to be served by Jesus so we may, in turn, obey Him and serve others. We honor Him by receiving all that He is and has obtained for us in Himself, not by giving Him what we think He needs or wants.

Some may ask at this point, How then do we properly "serve" God in light of passages that speak of us as His servants? We must begin by defining what it means to be God's servants. We are lovingly called God's "servants" because He redeemed us and now we belong to Him. We have been bought with a price—the blood of Jesus (1 Cor. 6:20). We are also properly called God's "servants" inasmuch as we submit to His authority and recognize His right to tell us to do whatever pleases Him.

However, we need to realize that every command from the Father is His way of telling us how much He wants to serve us. The pathway of holiness and obedience is the place where He meets us to carry our burdens and give us the power to do His will. The Father doesn't need our help. He requires our obedience and offers His help.

We all need to learn to live by the Father's grace and power. The key is simply yielding to His Spirit, who indwells you. Do you realize that for every work of the flesh mentioned in Galatians 5:19–21, there is an opposite fruit of the Spirit that can be manifested in its place? In every situation you have a choice. Will you yield to self-will, or will you yield your will to the Father's will? Yielding is an attitude of the heart. It's not so much a question of *doing* anything as much as it is *submitting* to the Spirit when He wants to live the Christian life through you. If you will yield to Him, the Holy Spirit will supply the grace and power to overcome. All He wants is your heart.

We are not going to make it to the end simply because

we're a bunch of spiritual hotshots. We are not even going to make it because we are great followers. We are going to make it because He's a great Father and leader!

The radical call to holiness is really an invitation to let the beauty and sweetness of Jesus so fill our hearts and minds that the seductive pleasures of sin will be swallowed up in the holy satisfaction of His presence.

CAPTURED BY A SWEETER SOUND

In his book *Pleasures Evermore* Sam Storms uses the story line of an ancient legend to graphically illustrate how the seductive pleasures of sin can be overcome in each of our lives:

> Most of you will remember the story from Greek mythology of Odysseus, also known as Ulysses. Having kissed his tearful wife, Penelope, good-bye, he set sail from his much-beloved home of Ithaca, destined for the city of Troy. The reason for his journey was that Paris, the prince of Troy, had seduced (or stolen) Helen, the wife of Menelaus, king of Greece. Menelaus, together with his brother Agamemnon, Ulysses, and a mighty Greek army, undertook the daunting task of recapturing Helen and restoring dignity to their beloved Greece. Hiding in the belly of a Trojan horse, Ulysses and his men gained access to the city, slaughtered its inhabitants, and rescued the captive Helen (she whose "face launched a thousand ships"). The return voyage to Ithaca, however, would prove far more daunting.
>
> Much could be said of Ulysses' encounter with the witch Circe and his careful navigation between the treacherous Scylla and Charybdis. Hollywood has done an admirable job of portraying for us the adventures of our Greek hero. My fascination,

however, has always been with the infamous Sirens. Countless were the unwitting sailors who, on passing by their island, succumbed to the outward beauty of the Sirens and their seductively irresistible songs. Once lured close to shore, their boats crashed on hidden rocks lurking beneath the surface of the sea. The demonic cannibals whose alluring disguise and mesmerizing melodies had drawn them close wasted little time in savagely consuming their flesh.

Ulysses had been duly warned about the Sirens and their lethal hypocrisy. Upon reaching their island, he ordered his crew to put wax in their ears lest they be lured to their ultimate demise. "Look neither to the left nor right," he commanded them. "And row for your lives." Ulysses had other plans for himself. He instructed his men to strap him to the mast of the ship, leaving his ears unplugged. "I want to hear their song," said the curious, but foolish, leader. "No matter what I say or do, don't untie me until we are safely at a distance from the island."

Ulysses was utterly seduced by the songs of the Sirens. Were it not for the ropes that held him fast to the mast, Ulysses would have succumbed to their invitation. Although his hands were restrained, his heart was captivated by their beauty. Inwardly he said Yes, though outwardly the ropes prevented such indulgence. His No was not the fruit of a spontaneous revulsion but the product of an external shackle.

Such is the way many live as Christian men and women. Their hearts pant for the passing pleasures of sin. They struggle through life saying No to sin, not because their hearts are so inclined but because their hands have been shackled by the laws, rules, taboos, and prohibitions of their religious environment. Their obedience is not the glad product of a transformed nature but a reluctant conformity born of fear and shame. Is that the way you want to live? How do you account for your "obedience"? Are you bound tightly to the mast of religious expectations, all the while wanting to do the opposite of what is done? Is there not a better way to say No to the sinful sounds of Sirens?

Jason, like Ulysses, was himself a character of ancient mythology. Again, like Ulysses, he faced the temptation posed by the sonorous tones of the Sirens. But his solution was of a different order. Jason brought with him a certain Orpheus, the son of Oeager. Orpheus was a musician of incomparable talent, especially on the lyre and flute. When it came time, Jason declined to plug the ears of his crew. Neither did he strap himself to the mast to restrain his otherwise lustful yearning for whatever pleasures the Sirens might sing. Instead, he ordered Orpheus to play his most beautiful, most alluring songs. The Sirens didn't stand a chance! Notwithstanding their collective allure, Jason and his men paid no heed to the Sirens. They were not in the least inclined to succumb. Why? Because they were captivated by a transcendent sound. The music of Orpheus was of a different order. Jason and his men rebuffed the sounds of the Sirens because they had heard something far sweeter, far more noble, far more soothing.

It is only for you to answer. No one can choose on your behalf. The options are clear. Will you continue to fight against the restrictive influence of legal ropes and the binding power of fear, reprisal, and guilt, while your heart persists in yearning for what your hand is denied? Or do you long to shout a spontaneous and heartfelt No! at the Sirens because you've heard a sweeter sound?[8]

You must allow the sweeter sound of Jesus to capture your heart so you can say no to the seductive sounds of this world.

CLOSING PRAYER

Father, continue to reveal Your heart to me. I don't have all the words to express my gratitude for the incredible things You have done. Your grace is more than amazing. Part of me is homesick, because I so long to be with You and enjoy You forever. I ask You to unveil Your heart to me. Infuse fresh hope. Captivate me with Your passion. And stir within me a fresh desire for You. Empower me to walk righteously all the days of my life. In Jesus's name.

The Father uses hunger born out of desperation to wean us from the world and make us addicted to Him.

persevering in our quest for intimacy

chapter 8

Enjoying God is all about intimacy with God. It's about knowing Him and being known by Him. It's experiencing His love and responding to it. It's serving Him out of a sincere desire to please Him because He is the supreme pleasure of your life.

Throughout this book I've been laying a foundation to help you understand God's enormous passion for you. It's clear from Scripture that serving God is not the ultimate reason you were born. You were born for intimacy with the Father. The nearness of God to your heart is the crowning glory of your life on the earth! There's nothing more fulfilling than experiencing the tangible, manifest presence of the Father.

In this last chapter I want to share some practical ideas on how to cultivate intimacy with the Father. In so doing, I hope to encourage you in your quest to enjoy Him. However, you need to understand that no one can really instruct you in a relationship with God. While I can give you certain tips and share lessons that I've learned during my spiritual journey, you must experience God personally.

It's like marriage. You can read a hundred books on the subject, but until you've said "I do" and walked it out over time, you really don't know what it's like to be married. It's different for everyone.

So I'm going to offer you some valuable insights that will hopefully stimulate your appetite for a deeper relationship with the Lord. I'll provide enough information for you to begin your journey, but you'll have to venture into new realms of experiencing God for yourself. Ultimately you are the one who will have to hunger and thirst for richer encounters with Him.

Although I've already mentioned several times that it takes God to pursue God—that it takes the Father's initiative to stir one's heart to holy passion—you also have a part to play. There will be times in your Christian walk when you will have to persevere in your quest for intimacy with God. This is when you will need to understand the value of opening your heart to His desire for you.

THE PERSISTENT QUEST

Persistence in wanting to experience the Lord in deeper, heartfelt ways will always be honored. In Luke 18:2–8 Jesus told the story of a judge who neither feared God nor cared about men, but because a widow was relentless in asking for justice against an adversary, the judge responded to her plea. In verse 7 Jesus said, "And will not God bring about justice for his chosen ones, who cry out to him day and night? Will he keep putting them off?"

If God responds faithfully to those who seek justice, how much more will He respond to those who want to know Him more intimately? God has an even greater hunger and passion in His heart for you than you have for Him. He's always seeking to draw you closer to Himself in very tangible, real ways.

Deep is forever calling to deep. It's a continuous, unfolding process, but you must respond. You must persist in your yearning for Him, knowing that in due time the longing of your heart will be satisfied beyond anything you could ever imagine.

One of the greatest evidences of humility is seen when a person feels broken, empty, and dry but says to the Father, "In spite of all the hassles I'm experiencing, You are worth everything. I'm going to keep opening up my heart and mind to Your love until You reveal Yourself to me in deeper ways."

I believe the Father looks for opportunities to reward the heart that refuses to be denied. Need proof? Look at the life of Jacob. Many sermons have given Jacob a bad rap. He's usually called a conniver and sneak for tricking his brother, Esau, out of his birthright. But will you consider looking at this story from a different perspective?

Nowhere in the Bible will you ever find God bad-mouthing Jacob. In fact, it was God who renamed him "Israel." As I've searched the Scriptures, I've become convinced that Esau never had a heart for his birthright. That doesn't mean I excuse everything Jacob did. But I believe there was something about the cry of Jacob's heart that God loved.

Esau sold his birthright—namely, everything that had been promised his grandfather Abraham—in a moment of weakness to gratify his flesh. Who wanted the birthright more? Jacob did. The Bible is clear that Esau despised his birthright. He treated it lightly. Jacob merely seized the opportunity of the moment to embrace what Esau didn't want in the first place. In spite of Jacob's methods, we can learn something from the persistence he demonstrated.

Jacob yearned for the birthright. He had a heart for the fullness of all that was promised his brother. Under the new covenant we should have a heart like Jacob's that longs for our birthright in Christ—all that He is and all that He represents. We should pray for a holy tenacity that would cause us to say with Jacob, "I will not let go of Him until He blesses me."

I'm not simply talking about embracing the blessings that come from His hand; I'm talking about beholding His face, experiencing Him, and having our hearts so warmed and stirred that we become more passionate lovers of God than we've ever been before.

Because Jacob had a heart to wrestle with the preincarnate Christ, his name was changed from "Heel Grabber" to "One Who Prevailed With God." Wouldn't you like to have a name change like that? Are you willing to persevere in your quest for intimacy with the Father? We are so used to instant coffee, microwave popcorn, and fast-food restaurants that we have a hard time waiting for anything.

Over the years I've watched people begin their journey of intimacy with God and then quit because they didn't get what they wanted soon enough. They returned to their busy lifestyles and filled their hearts with other things because the journey didn't meet their expectations. God's manifest presence didn't overwhelm them as they had wanted, and so they gave up. They weren't willing to persist. They didn't continue to long for a greater revelation of their Father's love.

Ask Jacob if it was worth it to persevere and wrestle with God. I think you know what his answer would be. There are deeper realms in the heart of the Father than most believers have ever dreamed of, and they're available to you. You can experience as much of God as you want. Those who persist in their desire to know Him more will never be disappointed!

Have you ever noticed that some Christians experience a much closer intimacy with the Father than others do? Does God play favorites, or is there something else at issue here?

I believe that both Scripture and experience suggest that we are the ones who determine the depth of intimacy that we enjoy with the Father. At this very moment we are as close to Him as we've chosen to be.

This truth is clearly illustrated for us in the New Testament in the lives of Jesus's disciples. We find varying levels of intimacy even within their ranks. Among His early followers Jesus chose seventy and sent them out two by two to minister for Him. Later He chose twelve to be with Him and learn His ways. Within the twelve there emerged a circle of three with whom Jesus became especially close. They were privileged to observe things that the other nine disciples never experienced. Peter, James, and John were with Jesus at the raising of Jairus's daughter from the dead (Luke 8:51). They were allowed to behold His glory on the Mount of Transfiguration (Matt. 17:1). They were even honored to be with Jesus during His night of agony in the Garden of Gethsemane (Matt. 26:37).

Yet within the circle of three, there was one who took advantage of the opportunity to lean on Jesus's chest. It was love and desire that drew John into a deeper intimacy with Jesus than the other disciples seemed to experience. Jesus loved them all, but it was John alone who referred to himself as "the disciple whom Jesus loved."

I once heard of a woman who was meditating on the image of the apostle John leaning on Jesus's breast (John 13:25). She said to the Lord, "It just doesn't seem fair that John was the only disciple who got to lean on Your chest and hear Your holy heartbeat." She felt the Lord respond by saying, "John was the only one who wanted to."

The heartbeat of Jesus is still available to anyone who wants to live in His embrace. And that's what this book is all about. It's not about experimenting with the idea of enjoying God. It's about having an intense desire to go after the deepest relationship with God that is humanly possible. It's a call to a lifestyle of persevering in our quest for intimacy with the Father. There will always be those believers who refuse to be denied the highest things of God. They won't settle for anything less. I believe you're one of them. That's why you must persist. God will reveal Himself to those who truly have a heart for Him.

UNLEARNING A LIFESTYLE

Knowing God in deeper intimacy doesn't just come in what we learn but in what we have to unlearn. Experiencing Him in greater intimacy often means changing our lifestyle. It means learning to respond to Him differently. Encountering the Lord isn't hard; it's simply foreign to us. It's not that it's difficult; it's just different.

In Western society especially, we are continually tempted to try to squeeze the Father into the busyness of our lives. Why do you think there are so many "fifteen-minutes-with-God" type books on the market? Did you know that devotionals have grown into a $50-million-a-year market? With the various demands placed upon us by our culture, the Father is relegated to a brief quiet time in the morning or during lunch break, rather than being a companion with whom we dialogue throughout the day. God becomes someone who is allowed to stop in rather than abide. He's permitted to make an appearance but not steal the show.

Unlearning busyness is one of the most difficult things to deal with, because the quest for intimacy with God goes against all of our cultural conditioning. Something in the human makeup feeds off busyness. It allows us to feel good about ourselves. This is due in part to the fact that we believe we're successful only if we've accomplished something. But

God isn't sitting in heaven with a report card in one hand and a red marker in the other. He isn't waiting for you to complete a list of tasks. He didn't create you for that. He just wants to be with you.

In Luke 10 we are introduced to the story of Jesus visiting His friends Mary and Martha. Verses 38–40 say, "As Jesus and his disciples were on their way, he came to a village where a woman named Martha opened her home to him. She had a sister called Mary, who sat at the Lord's feet listening to what he said. But Martha was distracted by all the preparations that had to be made. She came to him and asked, 'Lord, don't you care that my sister has left me to do the work by myself? Tell her to help me!'"

In verses 41–42 we read Jesus's response: "'Martha, Martha,' the Lord answered, 'you are worried and upset about many things, but only one thing is needed. Mary has chosen what is better, and it will not be taken away from her.'"

I appreciate Martha's compassion as a servant. She knew what needed to be done. She was a faithful servant, but the things she worried about diverted her attention from Jesus. Martha represents a lot of good Christians who are involved in compassionate service but who don't take the time to sit at Jesus's feet.

Mary, on the other hand, represents those who are feeding on Jesus rather than only trying to feed Jesus. This simple principle is carried over into life and ministry even today—you can't feed others if you're not first feeding on Jesus. Ministry isn't just about preaching sermons or being involved in acts of service; it's about imparting life to others. You can't give out what you haven't first received and experienced yourself.

Once you capture the flavor of what Jesus said to Martha,

it becomes obvious that there's only one thing that ultimately matters in life—it's sitting at the feet of Jesus and being bathed in His love.

When we begin to respond to the Lord because of His love for us, we will discover a completely different lifestyle than what we've experienced before. One of the reasons is that we've never really known what it is to wait on the Lord. The invitation in Psalm 46:10 to "Be still, and know that I am God" sounds simple enough, but putting it into practice takes genuine effort.

I remember reading that verse years ago while studying the great saints and what they had to say about contemplation and silence. I thought, "Man, this sounds good! I think I'll try it." I remember sitting at His feet, trying to be quiet before Him, and finding my mind wandering in all directions. I began thinking about all the people I needed to call. I thought about the weather. I even thought about how I could improve my golf game. I was thinking about everything except God. That's when I realized that focusing on Him can be a struggle. It's not about religious striving, but it does take deliberate and diligent effort. In a very real sense, the fight of faith is the fight to stay satisfied with God. You have to work at staying satisfied with the Father, because even good things are going to compete for your time and attention.

Over the last few years the Father has been gradually weaning me from busyness. I've always loved to travel and teach, but He has lightened my teaching schedule somewhat so I can spend more time with Him. It's been a difficult lesson to learn. I've had my good days and my not-so-good days. Over time I've learned that there's nothing as fulfilling as spending time with Him. It's rich, and it's deep! And it's during such times that His love is actually experienced by me in tender yet profound ways. The more I take the time to simply be with Him and receive from Him, the more I can give to others. Yes, service has its place, but it's intended to be birthed out of passion and intimacy with the Father.

FINDING OUR CHIEF JOY

If we're going to experience a deeper intimacy with the Father, He must also become our chief joy and primary reason for living. As long as He is just another relationship that we try to squeeze into our busy schedules, we'll never know greater intimacy with Him. He must become the primary pleasure of our lives.

In Deuteronomy 8:10–14 God warns, "When you have eaten and are satisfied, praise the LORD your God for the good land he has given you. Be careful that you do not forget the LORD your God, failing to observe his commands, his laws and his decrees that I am giving you this day. Otherwise, when you eat and are satisfied, when you build fine houses and settle down, and when your herds and flocks grow large and your silver and gold increase and all you have is multiplied, then your heart will become proud and you will forget the LORD your God, who brought you out of Egypt, out of the land of slavery."

In times of prosperity it's easy to forget the Father. Blessings and ease have a way of blinding us to our need for Him. While God will bless us with a lot of good things, we must not allow those things to capture our hearts. It's not so much about having things; it's about not being controlled by those things.

There are times when the Father will cause us to become dissatisfied with our *stuff* so He is able to give us more of Himself. Looking back on my own life, I realize more than ever before that when God weaned me from finding my identity in the ministry, it was one of the best things He ever did for me. Sure, it was hard. But I experienced Him in ways I had never known before.

In his book *The Pursuit of God,* A. W. Tozer wrote:

> When the Lord divided Canaan among the tribes of Israel Levi received no share of the land. God said to him simply, "I am thy part and thine inheritance," and by those words made him richer than all his brethren, richer than all the kings and rajas who have ever lived in the world. And there is a spiritual principle here, a principle still valid for every priest of the Most High God.
>
> The man who has God for his treasure has all things in One. Many ordinary treasures may be denied him, or if he is allowed to have them, the enjoyment of them will be so tempered that they will never be necessary to his happiness. Or if he must see them go, one after one, he will scarcely feel a sense of loss, for having the Source of all things he has in One all satisfaction, all pleasure, all delight. Whatever he may lose he has actually lost nothing, for he now has it all in One, and he has it purely, legitimately and forever.[1]

In the introduction to the book *Jesus Freak,* Tom White, director of the Voice of the Martyrs, writes:

> The greatest pressure on the Freak who stands up for Jesus is the thought that they are alone—the only one. That is a lie. When I was on trial in Cuba for the Gospel, with a machine gun behind me, the prosecutor made fun of me. I told him about Hebrews 12:1, which mentions the cloud of witnesses around us. He was upset when I mentioned the saints and angels around me. Before trial I had been placed in special,

cold cells with no furniture, no blanket, and no light. Cold air was blowing in above the door. Everything was taken from me. I began singing hymns and praise choruses. The guards got angry and pounded on the steel door with their fists. I was not destitute and alone. Second Corinthians 6:10 states that we can have nothing, yet possess everything. I fellowshipped with the Creator of everything.[2]

The Father wants to become your everything—your supreme joy and desire. Ask Him if there are any areas in your life that you need to give to Him. Release the cry of your heart, and let Him know that you want Him more than anything. Regardless of what you may have to commit to Him, believe me, it will be worth it.

SPIRITUAL HUNGER

It's no secret that Americans are overweight. While other countries struggle to provide enough food for their people, America lives in abundance. According to one report, even our pets are obese. Nearly one-third of the cats and dogs in this country are overweight. Obesity is considered by veterinarians to be the top health problem among pets.[3]

In an indulgent, overweight society, it's difficult for us to understand what Christ actually meant when He spoke of hungering and thirsting after spiritual things. The Jewish historian Josephus tells us that in 70 A.D., when the Roman legions destroyed Jerusalem, one mother actually killed her infant son and cooked him for food. What this woman did was unthinkable! Yet she did it out of an absolute desperation to survive.[4]

There is an unavoidable *spirit of desperation* that always accompanies hunger. I believe this was at the heart of Jesus's statement in Matthew 5:6 when He said, "Blessed are those who hunger and thirst for righteousness, for they will be filled."

There appears to be a divine principle woven throughout the Word of God that clearly suggests that God answers the cry of the desperately hungry. There's something about spiritual hunger that deeply moves the heart of the Father. Hunger is the one characteristic that makes an individual stand out in the kingdom of God.

In his book *Born After Midnight* A. W. Tozer writes:

> Hunger and thirst are physical sensations which, in their acute stages, may become real pain. It has been the experience of countless seekers after God that when their desires became a pain they were suddenly and wonderfully filled. The problem is not to persuade God to fill us, but to want God sufficiently to permit Him to do so. The average Christian is so...contented with his...condition that there is no vacuum of desire into which the blessed Spirit can rush in satisfying fullness.
>
> Occasionally there will appear on the religious scene a man whose unsatisfied spiritual longings become so big and important in his life that they crowd out every other interest....His yearnings carry him away and often make something of a nuisance out of him. His puzzled fellow Christians shake their heads and look knowingly at each other, but like the blind man who cried after his sight and was rebuked by the disciples, he "cries the more a great deal." And if he has not yet met the conditions or there is something hindering the answer to his prayer, he may pray on in the late hours. Not the hour of night but the state of his heart decides the time of his visitation.[5]

In my book *Personal Revival* I relate a story of a young man who, in his search for God, came to study at the feet of a wise man. One day the teacher took his pupil to a lake and led him out into shoulder-deep water. Placing his hands on the student's head, he suddenly pushed him under the water and held him there until the young man, in desperation, fought his way to the surface. In utter shock and confusion the student stared at the old man as if to ask, "What in the world are you doing?" The teacher, in response, looked at his pupil and said, "When you want God as much as you wanted air, you shall find Him."[6]

Smith Wigglesworth once said, "To hunger and thirst after righteousness is when nothing in the world can fascinate us so much as being near to God."[7]

The Father uses hunger born out of desperation to wean us from the world and make us addicted to Him. It's not surprising then that He allows us to go through various circumstances and situations that produce a cry of desperation from deep within our spirits. But His real purpose is to make us so lovesick that we'll want Him more than anything else. When our desire for Him is greater than we've ever experienced before, He will answer the cry of our hearts and make Himself known to us in ways we've never imagined.

THE DARK NIGHT OF THE SOUL

This truth is also beautifully illustrated for us in the Song of Solomon. When we interpret the story allegorically, we discover that on two separate occasions in the life of the bride, the Lord appeared to withdraw His manifest presence from her. In Song of Solomon 2:8–17, the Lord challenged her to come out of her comfort zone and partner with Him in ministry. He wanted to take her to a new level of maturity. But she was hesitant to do so because of the challenges that awaited her. So the Lord made it look like He removed His discernible presence from her (Song of Sol. 3:1). He wasn't angry with her; He was jealous for her.

The withdrawal of the Lord's manifest presence in the bride's life depicted her inability to feel His presence. It had nothing to do with the security of her relationship with Him but rather with her ability to sense His closeness to her.

Notice the bride's response to the Lord's loving correction. According to Song of Solomon 3:2, she said to herself, "I will get up now and go about the city, through its streets and squares; I will search for the one my heart loves." The Lord was looking for this response. He wanted her to pursue Him by rising up in the dark season of her life. He wanted her to rise up, not give up. He wanted her to desperately seek Him so she could take hold of Him in a new way. And guess what happened? According to verse 4 of the same chapter, she found the one her heart loved. She "held him and would not let him go." The Lord wooed her out of her comfort zone and then in His grace enabled her to experience Him in an extremely passionate way.

The Lord's fiery passion for us will also compel Him to lovingly correct us at times. His jealousy for us is a good jealousy. His affections for us are like a fire that consumes everything in our lives that could prevent us from experiencing more of Him.

There will be times when the Lord will appear to lift the sense of His presence from our lives in order to communicate various truths to our hearts. He may use such times to make us aware of our need for Him. He may also use such occasions to alert us to some specific problem in our hearts. He may even allow such times to awaken in us a deeper hunger for Him. Regardless of the reason, the results will be well worth it. As He did with the bride in the Song of Solomon, He will allow us to experience Him in a passionate new way.

There was also a second occasion in the young bride's life when she experienced the withdrawing of the Lord's manifest presence. According to Song of Solomon 5:6, it was during a time when she was pursuing a deeper obedience in her own life. Listen to her words: "I opened for my lover, but my lover had left; he was gone. My heart sank at his departure. I looked for him but did not find him. I called him but he did not answer." She had never gone through anything like this before. This season of her life was different from what she had gone through in Song of Solomon 3:1–2.

The bride's greatest desire had been to experience the presence of the Lord. Yet it looked like He hid Himself from her. He didn't leave her. It was just that His tangible presence wasn't being experienced by her. And this was her biggest test! Would she fervently pursue Him without feeling His presence? Would she faithfully obey Him regardless of how difficult the circumstances became? Was she seeking the Lord primarily for her own spiritual pleasure, or would she love Him for His own sake?

What complicated matters even more for the young bride was the fact that the Lord gave her no reason why she had to endure her season of spiritual darkness. But the "silence of the Lord" was a part of His training to cause the bride to become more lovesick.

This is something that will happen to every Christian whose heart is set on loving the Lord. We read in Isaiah 50:10, "Who among you fears the LORD? Who obeys the voice of His Servant? Who walks in darkness and has no light? Let him trust in the name of the LORD and rely upon his God" (NKJV).

When we first look at this verse, we immediately assume

it's referring to the lost. After all, it's talking about darkness. But the darkness Isaiah is speaking of isn't referring to the darkness of sin or even demonic darkness. It's a darkness that comes to those who are intimate with the Father.

Have you ever awakened one morning to find all of your spiritual feelings gone? You have no desire to pray, and even when you do pray, it doesn't seem to accomplish anything. You try to read the Bible, but all the words seem to blend together. Nothing seems to make sense.

You search your heart for answers but come up with none. You rebuke the devil and ask others to pray for you, to no avail. You even listen to your favorite Bible teacher, and yet nothing changes.

St. John of the Cross called this season of life "the dark night of the soul." It's a time when you can't sense the presence of the Lord. There's an unusual sense of emptiness and barrenness that comes with it. You go to church and surround yourself with "on-fire" people and come away feeling nothing. You decide to fast and pray more, thinking this will cut short the season of dryness. But even these things don't seem to help. Not even prayer and fasting can remove this difficult time in your life—because it's been initiated by the Father and not the devil.

What you are going through is not new. It has happened to every man or woman who has ever been used significantly by the Father. It happened to Moses as he found himself on the backside of the desert for forty years. It happened to Job. It happened to David when the bottom appeared to drop out of his world.

As a young man David had a prophetic word spoken over him by the prophet Samuel. Can you imagine? It was a promise of God, delivered by a well-known, respected, certified prophet of God. David was going to be king over Israel!

Soon after things began falling into place for young David. He ended up in the king's court and found favor with Saul. He played his instruments for the king and brought comfort to Saul's heart. Everything was going along smoothly for David until the day Saul became jealous of him and tried to kill him. David could no longer trust the king, so he fled for his life. He was pursued like a common criminal and was forced to hide in caves. All this came on the heels of the promise of God and what appeared to be David's ascent to the throne of Israel.

David eventually came to a point in his life when he wanted out of his "dark night." Sound familiar? He found himself struggling to believe that the prophetic word given to him by Samuel would ever come to pass. He wanted relief from his pain and disillusionment, so he took matters into his own hands. David knew Saul was terrified of the Philistine army, so the future king of Israel took Goliath's sword and escaped into Philistine territory.

In 1 Samuel 27:1 we read, "But David thought to himself, 'One of these days I will be destroyed by the hand of Saul. The best thing I can do is to escape to the land of the Philistines. Then Saul will give up searching for me anywhere in Israel, and I will slip out of his hand.'" At this point David was tired of desert communion. But what was actually happening? God was using this season in David's life to fashion a man after His own heart.

According to the Bible it appears that David went through his crucible for a number of years. But I believe it was out of his season of desperation that many of the heartfelt messages of the Psalms were birthed. This is why so many Christians can readily identify with David. The Psalms not only express the cry of David's heart but also the cry of every believer who longs to experience the nearness of God's heart during their "dark night of the soul."

The Father never abandoned David during his season of testing. Psalm 18:17–19 describes David's eventual deliverance from King Saul. Look at the words very carefully: "He rescued me from my powerful enemy, from my foes, who were too strong for me. They confronted me in the day of my disaster, but the LORD was my support. He brought me out into a spacious place; he rescued me because he delighted in me."

Think of it! God delighted in David even after he had retreated into Philistine territory. Yes, the Father continued to fine-tune and mature David's life, but He enjoyed him during his times of weakness and discouragement. How was that possible? The Father saw the sincerity of David's heart. He saw the willingness in David's spirit to obey Him. He knew that David still loved and desired Him.

David understood the heart of the Father in a way very few men ever have. Maybe this is why he was able to say, "As a father has compassion on his children, so the LORD has compassion on those who fear him; for he knows how we are formed, he remembers that we are dust" (Ps. 103:13–14).

Thank the Lord, He never gives up on us! When the darkness surrounds us and we have no idea which way is up or down, it's good to know that the Father still loves us. Even when it appears that He has abandoned us, He is actually calling us to a deeper place in Him. Although it seems He has withdrawn from us, He simply wants to see just how much we desire Him. He's waiting to see if we'll reach out to Him, without inspiration and goose bumps, and tell Him, "Father, You mean more to me than all the hassles with my weak flesh, the battles in my mind, the dull ache in my heart, and the demonic resistance that I'm feeling."

Remember, God answers the cry of the hungry. He will never bypass the one who refuses to be denied the deeper things of His heart. I recently spoke with a woman who was experiencing her dark night. She felt spiritually barren and a million miles from God. I asked her, "What is in your heart? What do you really want?" Tears began rolling down her cheeks. She looked at me and said, "In my heart, I want God more now than I ever have."

Do you realize what the Father was doing? He was using the difficult times she was going through to reveal Himself to her in a more intimate way. We hate the feeling of barrenness. We hate the struggles. We want to give birth to the purposes of God, but we don't like going through the birthing process. We believe we can't persist without feeling inspired, so we're tempted to give up and retreat into what we've always known. But we need to realize that those who are intimate with the Father today started out this very same way.

Let's remove the mystique surrounding this whole issue of "seeking God." Many of us believe that experiencing the Father in an intimate way is only for spiritual heavyweights. However, this is far from true. Experiencing the presence of God is not a matter of deserving anything. It's simply yearning to know Him out of your own barrenness. It's worshiping, praying, and meditating on the Word, even when we feel little or no inspiration. It's saying to the Father, "I'm struggling, but I really want to experience more of Your manifest presence."

There's no mystery to experiencing the Lord. It's about being real with Him. Keep doing what you're doing. If you think you're wasting time or you're not doing things the right way, you'll be tempted to quit. But the Father doesn't despise what you're doing, even if you're reaching for Him with little or no feeling. He counts the yearning of your heart as honorable and will answer you in due time.

Keep responding to the Father in faith, believing that He will eventually reward you. Remember, faith is the issue, not feelings of inspiration. Put yourself in a position where the Holy Spirit can produce a deeper hunger in your heart. Although you can't produce passion, He will honor your desire for Him and create the necessary hunger in you. He will give you all the hope you need to persevere in your quest for intimacy with Him.

You may justifiably ask, "Well, how long do I have to experience this?" I don't have a clue. I wish I did. What makes the process even more difficult is not knowing how long it's going to last. I know you're looking for answers, but the Father isn't interested in just giving you answers—He wants you to experience more of Himself.

What you're going through is divinely orchestrated. The Father is closer to you than you realize. Although it appears that He has taken a step back from you, always remember that He lives in you. That's why it's important to persist in your quest to know Him more and to trust Him even when hope is hard to grasp. Remember that the Father's love for you is more powerful than anything you're facing.

You probably won't always respond well to desert communion or your dark night of the soul. The things that bring you to the place of desperation will never be easy to face. They have a way of bringing unpleasant issues to the surface in your life. But God knew that long before He allowed these things to touch you. While man looks at the outward appearance and external factors of your life, the Father looks at your heart.

My advice is simple: trust Him and hang on. You won't offend Him or embarrass Him with your questions or struggles. The one who started the work in you will bring it to completion.

C. S. Lewis once wrote, "On the whole, God's love for us is a much safer subject to think about than our love for him. Nobody can always have devout feelings....But the great thing to remember is that, though our feelings come and go, his love for us does not."[8]

One of the main reasons we experience the dark night of the soul is so we can relate to others in need. Some of the most precious times of ministry that I've experienced have taken place when I was completely vulnerable and transparent with other people. Over the years many people have come into my office distressed over the fact they weren't experiencing the presence or voice of the Lord as they once had. They thought they were the only ones to go through this dark and lonely season. When I've confessed to them that I've had similar struggles, they've been encouraged to realize they were not second-class Christians. They understood that the dark night of the soul is a normal part of the maturing process.

When you're dealing with confused, lonely, hurting people, you can't touch their hearts with information alone. But when you get real with them and share your own pain, frustration, and feelings of failure, your honesty will motivate them to open up their hearts as well. Out of your own brokenness you'll be able to impart life to them, because you're sharing a part of yourself and not just something you read in a book. You'll be able to leave them with hope, because the Father walked you through your dark night and took you deeper into His heart than you had ever been before.

Sometimes all people need is a listening ear and a compassionate response. They need your friendship, a hug, an affirmation, a blessing, or a prayer. As you watch friends and family members pass through their dark night, you'll probably see them respond in some rather immature ways. That's OK. Give them grace. After all, how well did you handle your situation?

A student once told me that when he had not felt the presence of the Lord for a while, he became so frustrated that he sat on the edge of his bed, pounded his fists on the pillow, and cried out, "Oh, God, You've got to do something." He said he couldn't pray for anyone, not even himself. All he could do was let out a gut-wrenching cry!

We were eating lunch together when he shared this with me. I said to him, "You know, what you expressed was one of the deepest forms of prayer any human being could ever pray."

It wasn't eloquent. It wasn't nice and neat. It was simply deep calling to deep. Have you ever experienced this cry of desperation? Sometimes it can't even be articulated very well, but it's one of the most powerful forms of prayer, because it comes from your gut. It's real. It's honest. And the cry of your spirit will get the Father's attention more quickly than ten good deeds or a dozen religious formulas.

If you're experiencing a dark night, I encourage you to do what you can by the grace of God. You're not backslidden—you still have a heart that loves Him. You're just in a season that everyone experiences. During those times when you sense your barrenness and brokenness, have no feelings of inspiration, and still desire your Father in a more intimate way, He is deeply moved. Simple expressions of love and adoration from weak and broken people overcome His heart. They are precious in His eyes.

It's not the accuracy of your "seeking" but the yearning of your heart that moves the Father. It's not about how much time you think you have to spend with Him. It has nothing to do with whether or not you can carry a tune. It's not even about how well you think you're doing. It's your yearning for Him that He loves and honors. Think of it! All of us can experience intimacy with God.

Cultivating Intimacy

How do you practice the presence of God when you first get up in the morning feeling like a zombie? How do you go from school, a busy work environment, the mall, or the gym to waiting on God? If you find it difficult, then you're normal. Waking up in the morning and not feeling much of anything won't inspire you to spend time with the Father. Having to leave your fast-paced lifestyle long enough to meet with Him is also far from easy. We've been culturally conditioned to live with constant busyness, noise, and activity.

Transitioning into a time of intimacy is often difficult. The mind races. The to-do list grows. And often a little voice whispers, "You're just wasting your time."

But waiting on God is essential. It's worth the effort. Hebrews 4:1 challenges us not to fall short of entering into His rest. God promises that rest can come to our hearts as we are intimate with Him. But the rest that accompanies intimacy isn't an absence of discipline. Verse 11 of the same chapter admonishes us to "labour therefore to enter into that rest" (KJV). Resting in intimacy with the Father is the fruit of consistent discipline. It isn't about being regimented or legalistic. It's about continually longing to experience greater intimacy with the Lord. It's bringing our hearts and minds into a position to commune with Him.

So on a practical level, how do we do it?

One of the most effective ways to cultivate your relationship with the Father is to have a place that the two of you can call your own. It can be a place in your home—a certain room or place on the couch or the floor. It can be outdoors as well. A nearby wooded area, stream, open field, path, or street can become your place. Whatever the location, it needs to be an area where you can go just to be with Him.

Jesus had His favorite places in which to spend time with His Father. Luke 22:39 says, "Jesus went out as usual to the Mount of Olives, and his disciples followed him." It's clear that the Mount of Olives was a key place for Jesus in cultivating intimacy with His Father. As I've studied the lives of great saints, I've become even more convinced that each of us needs a special place of retreat so that when we come into that place, it will automatically remind us of why we're there.

A PLACE FOR INTIMACY

Once you retreat to the place that belongs to the two of you, you're going to need something to help calm your mind and emotions. You're going to find that your mind will be thinking about all the activities of the upcoming day, or it will still be racing from all the events of the past few hours. Often a small to-do list will begin building in your mind. In order to remove this distraction, keep a piece of paper and a pen nearby. Record the things you need to do on the paper so that your heart and mind will be free to commune with your Father.

One of the best things you can do is listen to good worship music. Some of you may prefer to play your guitar or the piano. Do whatever works for you. Music helps me focus on the Father. Even taking walks with Him helps me unwind from the events of the day. I love being outside! The important thing is to find something that will help calm your heart and mind and assist you in transitioning from life's racetrack to God's resting place.

You may also want to prayerfully ask the Father to help you in this matter. You can pray something like this: "Father, settle my mind so I can meditate on Your heart and Your holy purposes. Give me the grace during this time to focus my passions and my emotions on You. Father, remove the yokes of this world, and yoke me to Your eternal purposes. Energize me. Let this time be rich. I'm here to meet with You. Invade the recesses of my heart, and help me stay focused on You. Manifest Yourself to me not only in this place but also throughout the rest of the day. In Jesus's name."

As your mind begins to unwind, start to express words of love and adoration to the Father. You can do it aloud or under your breath. Your words don't have to be complex or even complete sentences. Express your heart to Him. Tell Him what you like about Him. Thank Him for the little things He's done in your life. As you worship, remember that He's not out there somewhere in the wild blue yonder. He lives inside you. Your body is His temple. Offer yourself as a resting place for Him, and tell Him that you want Him to be your resting place.

Eventually your mind and emotions will cooperate, and you'll be able to focus on the Father. How busy your day is or how hectic your day has already been may determine how quickly you can bring your mind into an attitude of worship. Be patient. It takes time to cultivate intimacy with the Father. But He's longing for fellowship with you as well. And He's not giving up any time soon, so neither should you.

Try to find times throughout the day to steal away with Him. In other words, run away with Him in your heart and mind while you're driving to and from work, riding in an elevator, waiting in the grocery checkout line, or working out on a treadmill. Your Father is in you and all around you, and His desire for you is unending. Bring your thoughts around to Him throughout the day. Express your love and adoration. Ask Him to bring you into a deeper awareness of

His presence until you find yourself living more and more in an attitude of prayer and worship.

Prayerful Meditation

Why do you read the Bible? Is it something you feel you're obligated to do before you can begin your day or turn off the lights at night? Meditating on the Word isn't about reading a certain number of verses or chapters in the Bible every day. Neither is it merely educational. While a systematic study of the Bible is a wonderful and necessary part of the Christian life, reflecting on the Scriptures isn't about gaining information—it's about transformation. If you want your times in the Word to truly change you, then you can't read the Bible like a textbook or the latest novel. You can't race through the Word and expect nuggets of truth to leap off the pages at you.

Meditating on the Word isn't meant to be an achievement; it's meant to be an experience. There may be times when you don't get beyond two or three verses. But don't let that bother you. Just as a passing glance at a beautiful painting will never be sufficient to reveal its secrets, speed-reading the Bible will never be rewarding. Like a great painting, the Word must be savored and absorbed in the depths of your heart. Reflecting on the Scriptures involves not only your mind but also your whole being. A person who truly meditates on the Word doesn't merely think about what he's reading. He experiences it!

I love meditating on the Scriptures. I love taking the Word and rolling it over and over in my mind, allowing it to bathe my heart and emotions. I enjoy picturing myself in the stories and taking in all the sights and sounds of the moment. I love reflecting on the Psalms until they become as personal as my own thoughts and feelings.

I also enjoy praying the Scriptures back to the Father as I allow the words to express the cry of my heart. For example, in Psalm 119:18 David prayed, "Open my eyes that I may see wonderful things in your law." Over the years I have made this my prayer as well. This has been my approach as I've meditated on the Word.

After a time of worship, when my mind and emotions are focused on the Father, I ask Him to make His Word come alive in my heart. I pray for Him to open my spiritual eyes so I can behold His beauty through the Scriptures. I remind myself continually that the Father has left me some inspiring love letters so I can know and love Him more intimately.

In your quest to cultivate intimacy with the Father, I also highly recommend journaling. I'm not talking about recording the events of the day but writing honestly and deeply about the things you feel the Holy Spirit is speaking to your heart. Write about your struggles as well as your victories. Give yourself the chance to ask some hard questions. Journaling should be reflective and an honest expression of your heart. Journaling will allow you to get in touch with your deepest feelings.

Another method for cultivating intimacy with God is the practice of silence. The Father is continually whispering to us, "Be still, and know that I am God" (Ps. 46:10). However, the idea is foreign to most of us. The thought of being silent unnerves us.

I remember the first time I tried to practice silence. I just about went nuts. I was the kind of person who always had to be around people. But the more I waited on the Lord, the easier it became. I now love to sit in the Father's presence. I love to focus on Him and allow Him to settle on me and speak to me.

Remember, it's His nature to manifest Himself. He wants

to be with you even more than you want to be with Him. He wants to speak to you. Open your heart to Him. Begin with short periods of time. Don't say anything. Just focus on the One who lives inside you. Reflect on the beauty of His heart. Contemplate His greatness. Occasionally you can whisper some words of love and devotion to Him. But the purpose of silence is to allow Him to settle on you and bathe you in His peace and love. Your heart was made for this.

The more you cultivate this aspect of communion with the Father, the easier it will become. It may be difficult at first, but you will eventually cherish it.

As I've shared my heart with you about cultivating intimacy with the Father, I want you to understand that these are just suggestions to help you in your journey. I don't always do the same things every day, and I want you to feel free to be creative. Don't do anything based on duty alone. Learn to delight in the lover of your heart. As a friend of mine always says, "It's going from 'got to' to 'get to.'" It isn't about doing something just because it's the Christian thing to do. It's all about relationship. We get to enjoy the Father. We get to rest in His love and feel the pleasure of His heart.

The Father is also looking for a resting place. "This is what the LORD says: 'Heaven is my throne, and the earth is my footstool. Where is the house you will build for me? Where will my resting place be?'" (Isa. 66:1). Does the Father have a resting place in your life?

A pastor from Argentina once told me about several people who were walking down the sidewalk in front of a church building in his city. The congregation was experiencing a real move of the Spirit of God. As these people walked past this building, they were overwhelmed by the presence of the Lord. They found themselves on the ground, unable to move. Several Christians saw them and carried them into the building, where they eventually gave their hearts to the Lord. Although this story may seem a bit outlandish, it made me realize just how much God jealously longs for a people in which to live. He is looking for a resting place in the hearts of men. I believe we're coming into a season of time when the Father is going to reveal Himself in such a way that He will capture the heart of a generation.

I want you to be a part of that. Open your heart to your heavenly Father. Let Him embrace you in His love. Let Him bathe your mind and emotions with His tender affections. He wants to be your heart's delight. He wants you to enjoy Him forever.

CLOSING PRAYER

Father, open my heart to the fullness of knowing You. Create in me a hunger and desire to experience more of You. I want to be a passionate lover. Help me to go deeper with You in all areas of my life. Remove the distractions. Remove the hindrances. Remove the things that stand between us so I can run after You with wholehearted abandonment.

I want to live for You. I love You. Mold me. Shape me. Form me. And carry me in the palm of Your hand so I may enjoy You forever. In Jesus's name.

Notes

INTRODUCTION

1. John Piper, *Desiring God* (Sisters, OR: Multnomah Publishers, 1996), 17–18.

CHAPTER 1
THE DRAWING OF THE HUMAN HEART

1. Blaise Pascal, *Pascal's Pensees*, trans. W. F. Trotter (New York: E. P. Dutton, 1958), 113.
2. "Waterspouts: Tornadoes Over Water," *USA Today*, March 21, 2000.
3. Brent Curtis and John Eldredge, *The Sacred Romance* (Nashville: Thomas Nelson, 1997), 83. Used with permission.
4. Julian of Norwich, *Revelations of Divine Love* (London: Methuen, 1911), 12.

CHAPTER 2
THE DIVINE ROMANCE

1. Augustine, *The Confessions of Augustine in Modern English*, trans. Sherwood E. Wirt (Grand Rapids, MI: Zondervan, 1977), 125.
2. Philip Yancey, *Disappointment With God* (Grand Rapids, MI: Zondervan, 1988), 103–104.
3. Søren Kierkegaard, *Philosophical Fragments*, trans. David Swenson (Princeton, NJ: Princeton University Press, 1962), 31–43, as quoted in Yancey, *Disappointment With God*, 103–104.
4. Curtis and Eldredge, *The Sacred Romance*, 77–78.
5. Mike Bickle, *The Pleasures of Loving God* (Lake Mary, FL: Charisma House, 2000), 74. Used with permission.
6. Thomas à Kempis, *The Imitation of Christ*, trans. Sherley-Price (London: Penguin, 1975), book 3, chapter 5, 98.
7. Darin Hufford, *The Misunderstood God* (Newbury Park, CA: Windblown Media, 2009), 53.
8. Rick Joyner, *Shadows of Things to Come: A Prophetic Look at God's Unfolding Plan* (Nashville: Thomas Nelson, 2001), 180.
9. Yancey, *Disappointment With God*, 71.
10. Douglas John Hall, *God and Human Suffering* (Minneapolis, MN: Augsburg, 1986), 156, as quoted in Yancey, *Disappointment With God*, 71.

CHAPTER 3
THE WOUNDED HEART

1.   Associated Press, "Christopher Robin Milne, 75, Pooh's Companion," *New York Times*, April 22, 1966, http://www .nytimes.com/1996/04/22/world/christopher-robin-milne-75-pooh-s -companion.html (accessed January 30, 2012).

2.   US Census Bureau, *Custodial Mothers and Fathers and Their Child Support: 2007*, referenced in Rahul Thadani, "Single Parent Statistics," Buzzle.com, April 21, 2010, http://www.buzzle .com/articles/single-parent-statistics.html (accessed January 30, 2012).

CHAPTER 4
THE AUDIENCE OF ONE

1.   Watchman Nee, *Ministering to the House or to God?* (Los Angeles: Living Stream Ministry, 1993), 1, 3–5, 9–10, 14. Permission requested.

2.   Gary Smalley and John Trent, *The Blessing* (Nashville: Thomas Nelson, 1986), 24.

CHAPTER 5
FINDING SIGNIFICANCE

1.   Carl Bernstein, "Bernstein on Hillary Clinton's Ambition," MSNBC.com, June 1, 2007, http://today.msnbc.msn.com/ id/18984501/ns/today-books/t/bernstein-hillary-clintons-ambition/ (accessed January 31, 2012).

2.   "The Impact on Our Children," *Common Sense and Domestic Violence*, January 30, 1998, referenced in FathersforLife .org, "Children of Divorce and Separation—Statistics," http:// fathersforlife.org/divorce/chldrndiv.htm (accessed February 1, 2012).

3.   Fatherless Homes, "Alienation and Fatherless Statistics," FathersSupportingFathers.org, http://www.fatherssupportingfathers .org/research.html (accessed February 1, 2012).

4.   Anthony DeMello, *The Way to Love* (New York: Doubleday, 1991), 64.

5.   Henry Nouwen, *In the Name of Jesus* (New York: Crossroad, 1989), 42.

6.   Max Lucado, *Come Thirsty* (Siloam Springs, AR: W Publishing Group), calendar published by Garborg's, a brand of DaySpring Cards, Inc.

CHAPTER 6
THE AFFECTIONATE AND APPROACHABLE FATHER

1. Floyd McClung, *Finding Friendship With God* (Ann Arbor, MI: Servant Publications, 1992), 149–150. Used with permission.

2. Martyn Lloyd-Jones, *Romans 8*, quoted in Ed Piorek and Tom Stype, *The Spirit of the Father* (1990), a teaching syllabus notebook, 7–8.

3. Ibid.

4. Charles Grandison Finney, *Charles G. Finney: An Autobiography* (Westwood, NJ: Fleming H. Revell, 1876, 1908), 20. Viewed at www.books.google.com (accessed February 2, 2012).

5. Ibid., 20–21.

6. James Gilchrist Lawson, *Deeper Experiences of Famous Christians* (Anderson, IN: Warner Press, 1911), 348.

7. C. Truman Davis, "A Physician Testifies About the Crucifixion," Study 197, http://www.giveshare.org/BibleStudy/197.crucifixion.html (accessed February 13, 2012). Used with permission.

8. Ibid.

9. Floyd McClung, *The Father Heart of God* (Eugene, OR: Harvest House, 1985), 111–114. Used with permission.

10. Abraham Joshua Heschel, *God in Search of Man* (New York: The Noonday Press, 1983), 74.

CHAPTER 7
LOVE-EMPOWERED HOLINESS

1. Jonathan Edwards, "Christian Happiness," in *The Works of Jonathan Edwards: Sermons and Discourses 1720–1723*, vol. 10, Wilson H. Kimnach, ed. (New Haven: Yale University Press, 1992), 303.

2. C. S. Lewis, *The Weight of Glory and Other Addresses* (New York: Touchstone, 1996), 25–26.

3. John Piper, *Future Grace* (Sisters, OR: Multnomah Books, 1995), 9.

4. Brennan Manning, *Abba's Child* (Colorado Springs, CO: NavPress, 1994), 117–118. Used with permission.

5. Joachim Jeremias, *The Parables of Jesus* (New York: Charles Scribner and Sons, 1970), 84.

6. Brian D. McLaren, *A New Kind of Christianity* (New York: Harper One, 2010), 205.

7. Roxanne Brandt, *Ministering to the Lord* (Springdale, PA: Whitaker House, 1973), 14–16.

8. Sam Storms, *Pleasures Evermore* (Colorado Springs, CO: NavPress), 104–106. Used with permission.

CHAPTER 8
PERSEVERING IN OUR QUEST FOR INTIMACY

1. A. W. Tozer, *The Pursuit of God,* (Camp Hill, PA: Christian Publications), 19–20.

2. dcTalk and the Voice of the Martyrs, *Jesus Freaks* (Tulsa, OK: Albury, 1999), 13. Used with permission.

3. Corey Binns, "Obesity Epidemic Strikes Pets, Too," May 3, 2007, LiveScience.com, http://www.livescience.com/4436-obesity-epidemic-strikes-pets.html (accessed February 14, 2012).

4. Flavius Josephus, *The Wars of the Jews* 6.3.4. Numbers reference book, chapter, and section number. Viewed at http://www.bible.ca/pre-flavius-josephus-70AD-Mt24-fulfilled.htm (accessed February 24, 2012).

5. A. W. Tozer, *Born After Midnight* (Camp Hill, PA: Christian Publications), 8–9.

6. S. J. Hill, *Personal Revival* self-published; to order, visit www.sjhillonline.com.

7. W. Hacking, *Smith Wigglesworth Remembered* (Tulsa, OK: Harrison House, 1981), 78.

8. Rabia al-Adawiyya, Sherwood E. Wirt, and Kersten Beckstrom, eds., *Living Quotations for Christians* (New York: Harper & Row, 1974), no. 1163.